D0985911

hide
this
japanese
phrase
book

INSIDE

INTRO

So, you're going to visit Japan, huh? Well then, you'd better learn a couple of useful phrases. By "useful" we mean the lingo you need to hook up, check in, and hang out. This un-censored phrase book's got you covered with everything you need to speak cool Japanese — saying hi, getting a room, spending your bucks, finding a cheap place to eat, scoring digits... and a helluva lot more. We've even thrown in a few totally offensive, completely inappropriate, and downright nasty terms — just for fun. You'll be able to easily spot these by looking for ❗.

We've got your back with insider tips, too. Check these out for up-to-date info that'll help you maneuver around a Japanese locale...

FACT   cool facts that may seem like fiction

the scoop   tips on what's hot and what's not

yo!   info you've gotta know

Warning ❗ — this language can get you into trouble. If you wanna say it in public, that's up to you. But we're not taking the rap (like responsibility and liability) for any problems you could encounter by using the expressions in this book. These include, but are not limited to, verbal and/or physical abuse, bar brawls, cat fights, arrest... Use caution when dealing with Japanese that's hot!

SPEAK JAPANESE – THE EASY WAY

This book will not make you an expert in Japanese, but it will help you get through your stay without sounding like a loser when speaking the language. To make it easy for you, we've provided really simple phonetics (those letters right under the Japanese expressions) with every entry you could say out loud. Just read the phonetic guide throughout this book as if it were English! But if you must sweat over the nitty-gritty details of the pronunciation system we've used, here's a quick guide.

Japanese Script	Pronunciation	English Equivalent
あ	as in f**a**ther	a
い	as in **i**mitate	i
う	as in c**u**shion	u
え	as in **e**lephant	e
お	as in **o**range	o
か	as in **ka**rate	ka
き	as in **ki**ss	ki
く	as in **cu**shion	ku
け	as in **ca**ble	ke
こ	as in **co**ma	ko
さ	as in **Sa**hara	sa
し	as in **shi**lling	shi

Japanese Script	Pronunciation	English Equivalent
す	as in **su**e	su
せ	as in **sa**vvy	se
そ	as in **so**	so
た	as in **ta**r	ta
ち	as in **chi**lly	chi
つ	as in **zu**	tsu
て	as in **te**mple	te
と	as in **to**mato	to
な	as in **na**ive	na
に	as in **ni**bble	ni
ぬ	as in **no**odle	nu
ね	as in **ne**t	ne
の	as in **No**rway	no
は	as in **ho**ney	ha
ひ	as in **he**	hi
ふ	as in **hoo**ligan or **fu**ll	hu / fu
へ	as in **he**reditary	he
ほ	as in **ho**t	ho
ま	as in **ma**rgarine	ma
み	as in **mi**racle	mi

Japanese Script	Pronunciation	English Equivalent
む	as in **moo**	mu
め	as in **me**rry	me
も	as in **mo**re	mo
や	as in **ya**rd	ya
ゆ	as in **you**	yu
よ	as in **yaw**ning	yo
ら	as in **ra**ther or **la**ther	ra / la
り	as in **ri**pple or **li**ttle	ri / li
る	as in **ru**le or **lu**minous	ru / lu
れ	as in **re**d or **le**tter	re / le
ろ	as in **ro**ster	ro
わ	as in **wo**bble	wa
を	as in **oh**	o
ん	as in su**ng**	n

THE BASICS

hi there

Make a good impression on the locals from the get-go.

Hello!
こんにちわ!
kon'nichiwa
Formal yet friendly.

Hi!
やあ!
yaa
Cute and to the point.

Hi, how are you?
やあ、お元気ですか?
yaa, ogenki desu ka

Good evening.
こんばんわ。
konbanwa

how're you doin'?

Ask about someone's well-being.

How are you?
お元気ですか?
ogenki desu ka

What's up?
元気?
genki

How's it going?
最近どうですか?
saikin doodesu ka

Doing well?
元気?
genki

the
scoop

When meeting someone for the first time, knowing the right body language is just as important as saying the right phrases.

It's polite to bow when you meet or say goodbye to a Japanese person. But it's not necessary to do a 90-degree bow or to bow excessively. Take note that it is impolite to eyeball the other party when bowing — unless you want to challenge the person to a Karate or Judo match! However, it is also common to shake hands when you meet someone or say goodbye.

hey you!
Wanna get someone's attention? Try these.

Excuse me!	すみません！ *sumimasen*
Yo!	よお! *yoo* *A quick way to get someone's attention.*
Hey!	おい! *oi*

FACT

The most common form of address is "san". Simply add the word "san" after the person's last name. (It doesn't matter whether the person is a man or a woman; it's "san" for everyone!) For example, "Suzuki-san"; "Tanaka-san". You may add "kun" after a man's first name, or "chan" after a woman's first name, if the person is your friend and about same age or younger than you. For example, "Kazuo-kun" and "Aya-chan".

sorry

Oops...need to apologize?

My bad.	私のミスです。
	Watashi no misu desu
Excuse me!	すみません!
	Sumimasen
Sorry!	ごめんね!
	Gomen ne
I'm sorry	ごめんなさい!
	Gomen nasai
I'm truly very sorry.	本当にごめんなさい!
	Hontoo ni gomen nasai
I was bad.	私が悪かったです。
	Watashi ga warukatta desu
I didn't mean to do that.	そんなつもりはありませんでした。
	Son'na tsumori wa arimasendeshita

huh?

What did he or she just say? Make sure you understood it correctly.

Do you speak English?	英語を話せますか?
	Eigo o hanasemasu ka
What was that?	えっ、何ですか?
	Ett, nandesu ka
Could you spell it?	書いてくれませんか?
	Kaite kuremasen ka
Please write it down.	書いてください。
	Kaite kudasai
Can you translate this for me?	これを訳してくれませんか?
	Kore o yakushite kuremasen ka

I understand / I don't understand.	分かります/ 分かりません。 *wakarimasu / wakarimasen*
Do you understand?	分かりますか? *wakarimasu ka* *Let's hope someone has a clue to what's going on!*
Can you repeat that?	もう一度言ってくれませんか? *moo ichido itte kuremasen ka*
Can you repeat slowly?	もう一度ゆっくり言ってくれませんか? *moo ichido yukkuri itte kuremasen ka*

help

Got yourself into a sticky situation?

Can you help me?	助けてください。 *tasukete kudasai*
Help!	助けて! *tasukete*
Call the police!	警察を呼んでください! *keisatsu o yonde kudasai*
Stop thief!	泥棒を捕まえてください! *doroboo o tsukamaete kudasai*
Fire!	火事です! *kaji desu*
I'm lost.	道に迷いました。 *michi ni mayoimashita*
Get a doctor!	医者を呼んでください! *isha o yondekudasai*

emergency

Just in case you get into trouble.

Where's the nearest police station?	最寄りの警察はどこですか？ *moyori no keisatsu wa dokodesu ka*
I want to report ...	...の届出をしたいのですが。 *... no todokede o shitai nodesuga*
an accident.	事故 *jiko*
an attack.	暴行 *bookoo*
a mugging.	強盗 *gootoo*
a rape.	レイプ *reipu*
a theft.	窃盗 *settoo*
I've been robbed.	強盗に遭いました。 *gootoo ni aimashita*
I've been mugged.	強盗に遭いました。 *gootoo ni aimashita*
I need to contact the consulate.	領事館に連絡する必要があります。 *ryoojikan ni renraku suru hitsuyoo ga arimasu*

FACT

In an emergency, dial 119 to talk to English-speaking operators. To get the police, dial 110. If you are using a public phone, push the red button before you dial 110 or 119, and the call is free.

the scoop

You can ask for directions at the nearest "koban" ('police box'), if you are lost. This mini police station is unique to Japan, and there's one in every neighborhood throughout the country. The police personnel will gladly help you out, but it's best to have the address of your destination written down, as they usually don't speak English.

bye-bye

From classic to cool, here are the best ways to say good-bye.

Good-bye.	さようなら。 *sayoonara*	
Bye!	じゃあね! *jaane*	
See you later.	また、あとで。 *mata, atode*	
See you soon.	じゃあ、また。 *jaa, mata*	
Good night.	おやすみなさい。 *oyasuminasai* *Say it when it's bedtime.*	

thank you!

Show someone your appreciation and gratitude.

Thank you!	ありがとうございます！ *arigatoo gozaimasu*
Thank you for your help!	ご親切にどうもありがとうございました！ *goshinsetsu ni doomo arigatoo gozaimashita*
Thank you very much indeed.	本当にありがとうございました。 *hontoo ni arigatoo gozaimashita*
I'm really grateful for your help.	助けてくださって、本当に感謝しています。 *tasukete kudasatte hontoo ni kansha shiteimasu*

by plane

Just arrived? Going somewhere? Act like you know what you're doing.

To ..., please.	...までお願いします。
	... made onegai shimasu

One-way. / Round-trip.	片道 / 往復
	katamichi / oofuku

How much?	いくらですか？
	ikura desu ka

Are there any discounts?	割引はありますか？
	waribiki wa arimasu ka
	Doesn't hurt to ask!

When is the (...) flight to ...?	...への（...の）便はいつですか？
	... eno (... no) bin wa itsu desu ka

(first)	最初
	saisho

(next)	次
	tsugi

(last)	最後
	saigo

I'd like ... ticket(s).	チケットを...枚ください。
	chiketto o ... mai kudasai

one	一
	ichi

two	二
	ni

Is there any delay on flight ...?	...便は遅れるのでしょうか？
	... bin wa okurerunodeshoo ka

How late will it be?	どれくらい遅れますか？
	dorekurai okuremasu ka

Which gate does flight ...leave from?	...便はどのゲートから出発しますか？
	... bin wa dono geeto kara shuppatsu shimasu ka
Where is / are ...?	...はどこですか？
	... wa doko desu ka
the baggage check	荷物検査
	nimotsu kensa
the luggage carts	荷物用カート
	nimotsu yoo kaato

the SCOOP

Need cheap airline tickets? Check with Japanese airlines such as JAL and ANA for any special promotions in advance if possible. The "Yokoso (Welcome) Japan" Airpass offers discounted fare on domestic flights for overseas travelers to Japan. Do your research online to get the details, as well as the terms and conditions. Alternatively, there are discount ticket providers such as Ai-ticket.com and travel agencies including JTB and H.I.S. offering a variety of special-priced travel packages (with air ticket and accommodation). The tourism peak periods are: late April to early May (Golden Week holiday), late July to August (summer holidays), and the end of the year (between Christmas and the New Year).

in flight

Sit back (if possible) and enjoy.

Can I have a blanket / pillow?	毛布 / 枕を持ってきてください。 *moofu / makura o mottekite kudasai*
I ordered a … meal.	...食を申し込んであったのですが。 *… shoku o mooshikonde atta nodesuga*
diabetic	糖尿病 *toonyoo byoo*
gluten free	無グルテン *mu-guruten*
kosher	コーシャ *koosha*
low calorie / cholesterol / fat / sodium	低カロリー / コレステロール / 脂肪 / 塩分 *tei karorii / koresuterooru / shiboo / enbun*
vegetarian	ベジタリアン *bejitarian*
I need a barf bag.	エチケット袋をください。 *echiketto bukuro o kudasai* *Gross.*

your stuff

Find it, grab it, and go!

Where is the luggage from flight …?	...便の荷物はどこですか？ *… bin no nimotsu wa dokodesu ka*
My luggage has been stolen.	私の荷物が盗まれました。 *watashi no nimotsu ga nusumaremashita*

My suitcase was damaged.	私のスーツケースが壊れています。
	watashi no suutsukeesu ga kowarete imasu
Our luggage hasn't arrived.	私たちの荷物が見つかりません。
	watashi-tachi no nimotsu ga mitsukarimasen
	What a nightmare.

the scoop

There are two airports in Tokyo: Narita International Airport, which handles mostly International flights, and Haneda Airport, handling mostly domestic flights. Narita Airport is located in Chiba prefecture, about 60 km outside Tokyo. The fastest way to get into Tokyo is via the Japan Railways (JR) Narita Express (NEX). The journey to the Tokyo Station takes about one hour and the fare is around 2,900 yen (one-way). Trains leave every 30 to 60 minutes.

by train

OK, first you gotta get there.

How do I get to the (main) train station?	（大きな）電車の駅までの行き方を教えてください。
	(ookina) densha no eki made no ikikata o oshiete kudasai
Is it far?	遠いですか？
	tooi desu ka

waitin' for the train

Learn to negotiate your way around the station.

Where is / are …?	…はどこですか？
	… wa doko desu ka
the bathroom	トイレ
	toire
the currency exchange office	両替所
	ryoogaejo
the baggage check	荷物検査
	nimotsu kensa
the lost-and-found	遺失物取扱所
	ishitsubutsu toriatsukaijo
the luggage lockers	荷物用ロッカー
	nimotsu yoo rokkaa

the platforms	**ホーム** *hoomu*
the snack bar	**軽食スタンド** *keishoku sutando*
Where is / are …?	**…はどこですか?** *… wa doko desu ka*
the ticket office	**切符売り場** *kippu uriba*
the waiting room	**待合室** *machiaishitsu*
Where can I buy a ticket?	**切符はどこで買えますか?** *kippu wa doko de kaemasu ka*
I'd like a (…) ticket to …	**…までの(…)切符をください。** *… made no (…) kippu o kudasai*
(one-way)	**片道** *katamichi*
(round-trip)	**往復** *oofuku*
How much is that?	**いくらですか?** *ikura desu ka*
Is there a discount for students?	**学生割引はありますか?** *gakusei waribiki wa arimasu ka*
Do you offer a cheap same-day round-trip ticket?	**同日往復割引切符はありますか?** *doojitsu oofuku waribiki kippu wa* *arimasu ka*
Could I have a schedule?	**時刻表をください。** *jikokuhyo o kudasai*
How long is the trip?	**どれくらいかかりますか?** *dorekurai kakarimasu ka*

When is the (…) train to …?	(…) 行きの … の電車はいつですか？
	(…) iki no … no densha wa itsu desu ka
(first)	最初
	saisho
(next)	次
	tsugi
(last)	最後
	saigo

the scoop

Japan's rail network is very well-developed. Japan Railways (JR) covers almost all parts of Tokyo. A dozen other private railway companies also operate their networks around the metropolitan areas. If you are staying in Tokyo, you can purchase the Suica or PASMO travel cards. These cards can be used on all trains, subways and buses in Greater Tokyo. For more information on Suica and PASMO, check out: www.japan-guide.com.

Tourists can also purchase JR passes for unlimited travel on almost all JR trains nationwide. There are 7, 14 and 21-days passes available. However, take note that you can only purchase them outside Japan. Check with Japan Airlines offices, travel agents, or your local Japan Travel Bureau (JTB) offices. For more information on the Japan Rail Pass, check out: www.japan-guide.co

FACT

The Shinkansen is Japan's world renowned Bullet Train. The trains travel at speeds of up to 188 mph, and provide links to most major cities in Japan. The Shinkansen is reportedly punctual to within six seconds of its scheduled arrival time. Looks like you'll have to look for other excuses if you are late in Japan!

train talk

Whether you're waiting for the train or looking for a seat, make conversation with a good-looking Japanese guy or girl.

Hello. Where is platform …?	こんにちわ。...番ホームはどこですか？ *kon'nichiwa. … ban hoomu wa doko desu ka*
Is this the train to …?	これは...行きの電車ですか？ *kore wa … iki no densha desu ka* *I bet you're hoping he/she will be on your train.*
Is this seat taken?	この席は空いていますか？ *kono seki wa aite imasu ka* *It may be a long ride—find someone to enjoy it with.*
Do you mind if I sit here?	ここに座ってもいいですか？ *koko ni suwattemo ii desu ka* *Get a little closer.*

by bus

It's not always the fastest way to get around, but it sure beats walking!

Where is the bus station?	バス乗り場はどこですか？ *basu noriba wa doko desu ka*

| Where can I buy tickets? | どこで切符を買えますか？ |
| | *doko de kippu o kaemasu ka* |

| A one-way / round-trip ticket to … | …までの片道 / 往復切符 |
| | *… made no katamichi / oofuku kippu* |

| A booklet of tickets. | 回数券 |
| | *kaisuuken* |

| How much is the fare to …? | …までの運賃はいくらですか？ |
| | *… made no unchin wa ikura desu ka* |

| Is this the right bus to …? | これは…行きのバスですか？ |
| | *kore wa … iki no basu desu ka* |

Could you tell me when to get off?	どこで降りるか教えてくれますか？
	doko de oriruka oshiete kuremasu ka
	Just in case you have no clue as to where you're headed…

Next stop, please!	次の停留所で止まってください！
	tsugi no teiryuujo de tomatte kudasai
	If you want the driver to stop, better say please!

by subway

Is goin' underground your style? Then you'll need these.

Where's the nearest subway station?	最寄の地下鉄の駅はどこですか？
	moyori no chikatetsu no eki wa doko desu ka
	Please let it be in walking distance.

| Where can I buy a ticket? | どこで切符を買えますか？ |
| | *doko de kippu o kaemasu ka* |

Could I have a map of the subway?	地下鉄の路線図をください。
	chikatetsu no rosenzu o kudasai
	If you ask nicely, you may actually get what you want.

Which line should I take for …?	...へはどの路線に乗ればいいのでしょうか？
	... e wa dono rosen ni noreba iinodeshoo ka
	If the subway map is incomprehensible, ask a cutie for help.

FACT

Subways networks in Tokyo and Osaka are notoriously complicated. Make sure you take some time to study and understand the networks and always have a JR route map with you.

the SCOOP

During rush hour, some carriages on the trains may be reserved for women only. Priority seats for the elderly and physically-disabled are available in almost every carriage and on buses.

| Is the next stop …? | 次の駅は...ですか？ |
| | *tsugi no eki wa … desu ka* |

Where are we?	ここはどこですか？
	koko wa doko desu ka
	Don't have a clue, huh?!

by taxi

Feelin' lazy? Get a cab.

| Where can I get a taxi? | どこでタクシーをひろえますか？ |
| | *doko de takushii o hiroemasu ka* |

Please take me to …	**…までお願いします。** *… made onegai shimasu*
a good bar.	**どこかいいバー** *dokoka ii baa*
a good club.	**どこかいいクラブ** *dokoka ii kurabu*
the airport.	**空港** *kuukoo*
the train station.	**駅** *eki*
this address.	**この住所** *kono jyuusho*
How much is that?	**いくらですか？** *ikura desu ka*
Keep the change.	**お釣りはいりません。** *otsuri wa irimasen*

FACT

Taxis are metered in Japan but it is good to ask for an estimated fare before you get in the car. Taxis in Japan are expensive, and may sometimes be less efficient than other forms of transport, especially during rush hour. Taxi fares usually start around 600-700 yen for the first two kilometers and increase by roughly 100 yen for every additional 500 meters traveled. In the late evening, rates increase by 20-30 percent. Taxis can be booked by phone for an additional fee.

the scoop

by car

Can't give up the luxury of having your own car?

Where can I rent a car?	レンタカーはどこで借りられ ますか？ *rentakaa wa doko de kariraremasu ka*
I'd like to rent ...	…を借りたいのですが。 *... o karitai nodesuga*
an automatic.	オートマチック車 *ootomachikku-sha*
a car with air conditioning.	エアコン付きの車 *eakon tsuki no kuruma*
How much does it cost per day / week?	1日 / 1週間につきいくらですか？ *ichinichi / ishuukan nitsuki ikura desu ka*
Is <u>mileage</u> / <u>insurance</u> included?	<u>走行距離無制限</u> / <u>保険</u>が含まれて いますか？ *<u>sookookyori</u> museigen / <u>hoken</u> ga fukumarete imasu ka*
Where's the next gas station?	次のガソリンスタンドはどこ ですか？ *tsugi no gasorin sutando wa doko desu ka*

Is it self-service?	セルフサービス式ですか？
	serufu saabisu shiki desu ka
Fill it up, please.	満タンにしてください。
	mantan ni shite kudasai

FACT

Driving in Japan is most daunting for any foreigner. Roads are narrow and congested, traffic rules and regulations are complicated, parking space is nearly impossible to find, and all the road signs are in Japanese! But for those who are undeterred, you will need a valid International Driver's license and you are only permitted to drive for up to a year after entering Japan.

car trouble

Having a breakdown?

My car broke down.	車が故障しました。
	kuruma ga koshoo shimashita
Can you send a <u>mechanic</u> / <u>tow truck</u>?	<u>整備士</u> / <u>レッカー車</u>を派遣してください。
	<u>*seibishi*</u> / *rekkaa sha o haken shitekudasai*
I've run out of gas.	ガス欠です。
	gasu ketsu desu
	Duh!
I have a flat.	タイヤがパンクしました。
	taiya ga panku shimashita
I've locked the keys in the car.	車のキーを閉じ込めてしまいました。
	kuruma no kii o tojikomete shimaimashita
	Nice one.

auto wreck

If you get pulled over or worse, these expressions may help.

He / She ran into me.	彼 / 彼女が飛び出してきました。
	kare / Kanojo ga tobidashite kimashita
He / She was driving <u>too fast</u> / <u>too close</u>.	彼 / 彼女の運転は<u>早すぎ</u> / <u>近すぎ</u>ました。
	kare / Kanojo no unten wa <u>hayasugi</u> / <u>chikasugi</u> mashita
I didn't see the sign.	標識を見ませんでした。
	hyoshiki o mimasendeshita
	Excuses, excuses.

by bike

Calling all bikers.

I'd like to rent …	…を借りたいのですが。
	… o karitai nodesuga
a bicycle.	自転車
	jitensha
a moped.	モペット
	mopetto
a motorbike.	オートバイ
	ootobai
How much does it cost per day / week?	1日 / 1週間につきいくらですか？
	ichinichi / ishuukan nitsuki ikura desu ka

3 MONEY

get cash

Get your yen and start spending your money!

Where's the nearest bank?	最寄りの銀行はどこですか？ *moyori no ginkoo wa doko desu ka*
Can I exchange foreign currency here?	ここで両替はできますか？ *koko de ryoogae wa dekimasu ka*
I'd like to change some dollars / pounds into yen.	ドル／ポンドを円に換えたいのですが。 *doru / pondo o en ni kaetai nodesuga*
I want to cash some travelers checks.	トラベラーズチェックを現金に換えたいのですが。 *toraberaazu chekku o genkin ni kaetai nodesuga*
What's the exchange rate?	為替レートを教えてください。 *kawase reeto o oshiete kudasai*

You can change money or traveler's checks at an 'authorised foreign exchange bank', major post offices and most large hotels. (You may need to present your travel documents during the transaction.) Take note that traveler's checks are not readily accepted outside the city areas.

It may be difficult to find private money changers in Japan. But the major department stores will usually have money changers in their premises.

ATM

Get cash fast.

Where are the ATMs [cash machines]?	ATM [現金自動預入支払機]はどこですか？ *ATM [Genkin jidoo azukeire shiharaiki] wa doko desu ka*

Can I use my card in the ATM?	私のカードはATM で使えますか？
	Watashi no kaado wa ATM de tsukaemasu ka
The machine has eaten my card.	私のカードがATMから出てこないのですが。
	Watashi no kaado ga ATM kara detekonai nodesuga

Many ATMs in Japan do not accept credit or debit cards issued outside Japan. But the ones found at the post offices and the 7-Eleven convenience stores do. (These ATMS also come with an English user interface.) You may have to pay an international 'ATM withdrawal fee'. Check what fees and daily or monthly limits are associated with international withdrawals, since these vary from bank to bank.

charge it

Can't figure out the currency exchange? Avoid the hassle and use your credit card.

Can I withdraw money on my credit card here?	ここはクレジットカードでお金を下ろすことはできますか？
	koko wa kurejitto kaado de okane o orosu koto wa dekimasu ka
Do you take credit cards?	クレジットカードは使えますか？
	kurejitto kaado wa tsukaemasu ka
I'll pay by credit card.	クレジットカードで支払います。
	kurejitto kaado de shiharaimasu

pay up

Here's how to part with your hard-earned dough.

How much is it?	いくらですか？ *ikura desu ka*
Do you accept travelers checks?	トラベラーズチェックは使えますか？ *toraberaazu chekku wa tsukaemasu ka*
Could I have a receipt please?	レシートをください。 *reshiito o kudasai*

HOTEL

get a room

You know you want to.

Can you recommend a hotel in …?	...でお勧めのホテルはありますか？ *… de osusume no hoteru wa arimasu ka*
Is it near the center of town?	それは街の中心に近いところにありますか？ *sore wa machi no cyuushin ni chikai tokoro ni arimasu ka* *You've gotta be close to the bars and clubs, right?!*
How much is it per night?	1泊いくらですか？ *ippaku ikura desu ka*
Is there anything cheaper?	もう少し安いところはありませんか？ *moo sukoshi yasui tokoro wa arimasen ka*
Could you reserve me a room there, please?	そこに予約を取ってくれませんか？ *soko ni yoyaku o totte kuremasen ka*
I have a reservation.	予約してあります。 *yoyaku shite arimasu*
My name is …	私の名前は...です。 *watashi no namae wa … desu*
I confirmed by e-mail.	Eメールで確認してあります。 *e-meeru de kakunin shite arimasu*
Could we have adjoining rooms?	続き部屋がいいのですが。 *tsuzuki beya ga ii nodesuga*

at the hotel

Need a room for tonight? Ask the right questions.

Do you have a room?	空き室はありますか？	
	akishitsu wa arimasu ka	
I'd like …	…に宿泊したいのですが。	
	… ni shukuhaku shitai nodesuga	
a single / double room.	シングル / ダブルルーム	
	singuru / daburu ruumu	
a non-smoking room	禁煙ルーム	
	kin'en ruumu	
a room with a bath / shower.	バス / シャワー付き客室	
	basu / shawaa tsuki kyakushitsu	

gotta have

Things you can't do without.

Does the hotel have …?	ホテルには...がありますか？
	hoteru niwa … ga arimasu ka
cable TV	ケーブルテレビ
	keeburu terebi
internet access	インターネットアクセス
	intaanetto akusesu
a gym	ジム
	jimu
a restaurant	レストラン
	resutoran
room service	ルームサービス
	ruumu saabisu
a swimming pool	プール
	puuru

a Wi-Fi® area	Wi-Fi®エリア
	Wi-Fi® eria
Is there … in the room?	客室には...がありますか？
	kyakushitsu niwa … ga arimasu ka
air conditioning	エアコン
	eakon
a phone	電話
	denwa
a TV	テレビ
	terebi

price

It all comes down to one thing.

How much is it …?	...いくらですか？
	… ikura desu ka
per night / week	1泊 / 1週間につき
	ichinichi / ishuukan nitsuki
Does the price include …?	料金には...は含まれていますか？
	ryookin niwa … wa fukumarete imasu ka
breakfast	朝食
	chooshoku
sales tax	消費税
	shoohi-zei
Do I have to pay a deposit?	保証金は必要ですか？
	hoshoo-kin wa hitsuyoo desu ka

problems

Tell 'em what's bothering you.

I've lost my key.	部屋の鍵をなくしました。 *heya no kagi o nakushimashita*
The lock is broken.	鍵が壊れています。 *kagi ga kowarete imasu*
The … doesn't work.	…が故障しています。 *… ga koshoo shite imasu*
fan	扇風機 *senpuuki*
heat	ヒーター *hiitaa*
light	電気 *denki*
There's no hot water. / There's no toilet paper.	暑いお湯が出ません。/ トイレットペーパーがありません。 *atsui oyu ga demasen. / toiretto peepaa ga arimasen*

FACT

Don't get burnt out. Eastern Japan (including Tokyo, Yokohama, Tohoku, and Hokkaido) uses the 100-volt, 50-cycle AC. Western Japan (including Osaka, Kyoto, Hiroshima, Shikoku, and Kyushu) uses the 100-volts, 60 cycle AC. If you're bringing your gizmos to Japan, check to see if you'll need a voltage converter. Electrical outlets in Japan fit two-pin plugs with flat blades.

necessities

More importantly...

Where's the bar?	バーはどこですか？ *baa wa doko desu ka* *This may be the most important* *expression in the entire book.*
Where's the swimming pool?	プールはどこですか？ *puuru wa doko desu ka*
Where are the restrooms?	トイレはどこですか？ *toire wa doko desu ka*
What time is the front door locked?	フロントドアは何時に閉まりますか？ *furonto doa wa nanji ni shimarimasu ka*
What time is breakfast served?	朝食は何時ですか？ *chooshoku wa nanji desu ka* *If breakfast is included, don't miss out!*
Could you wake me at ... please?	...時に起こしてください。 *... ji ni okoshite kudasai.*
Can I leave this in the hotel safe?	ホテルの金庫にこれを預けたいのですが。 *hoteru no kinko ni kore o azuketai* *nodesuga*
May I have an extra ...?	...を余分にいただけますか？ *... o yobun ni itadakemasu ka*
bath towel	バスタオル *basutaoru*
blanket	毛布 *moofu*
pillow	枕 *makura*

| roll of toilet paper | トイレットペーパー |
| | *toiretto-peepaa* |

Are there any messages for me?	私宛のメッセージはありますか？
	watashi ate no messeeji wa arimasu ka
	Waiting for that special someone to call?

ryokan

Japanese-style accommodation anyone?

| Do you have an extra futon? | 布団をもう一枚いただけますか？ |
| | *futon o moo ichi-mai itadakemasu ka* |

| Do you have yukata of a bigger size? | 大きいサイズの浴衣はありますか？ |
| | *ookii saizu no yukata wa arimasu ka* |

| Do you have slippers of bigger size? | 大きいサイズのスリッパはありますか？ |
| | *ookii saizu no surippa wa arimasu ka* |

| Where is public bath for gentlemen (ladies)? | 男性（女性）浴場はどこですか？ |
| | *dansei (Josei) yokujoo wa doko desu ka* |

| I need an extra washcloth for the bath. | お風呂用にタオルを余分に欲しいのですが。 |
| | *ofuro yoo ni taoru o yobun ni hoshii nodesuga* |

| What time is dinner served? | 夕食は何時ですか？ |
| | *yuushoku wa nanji desu ka* |

hostel

Looking for budget accommodations? The language you need is right here.

| Do you have any places left for tonight? | 今夜泊れますか？ |
| | *kon'ya tomaremasu ka* |

Do you rent bedding?	寝具は借りられますか？
	shingu wa kariraremasu ka
What time are the doors locked?	ドアは何時に閉まりますか？
	doa wa nanji ni shimarimasu ka
I have an International Student Card.	国際学生証を持っています。
	kokusai gakusei shoo o motteimasu

the scoop

You'll find that there's no shortage of 'alternative' accommodation in Japan, besides regular hotels.

There are more than 15,000 "minshuku" (family-run budget accommodation) in Japan. The "minshuku" are Japanese-style houses (with tatami rooms) found in the countryside. Breakfast is served. And sometimes dinner is provided as well. The host families usually don't speak much English, but they are known to be genuinely warm and friendly. Visit www.minshuku.jp/english/english html for more info. A night's stay typically costs between 6,000 to 8,000 yen. Take note that it is usually cash only at the "minshuku".

Also located in the countryside, but more expensive than the "minshuku", is the "ryokan". These are professionally-run inns with traditional Japanese rooms, serving exquisite Japanese meals. A night's stay in a "ryokan" could cost between 10,000 to 30,000 yen.

Those who are looking for a spiritual experience to go along with their holiday can give the "shukubo" (temple lodging) a try. You can stay at the "shukubo" regardless of your own religion, but you'll have to observe the regulations of the temple itself. Mount Koya (in Wakayama prefecture) has the largest "shukubo" clusters with about 50 temples offering lodging. The cost of a night's stay ranges from 5,000 yen to 15,000 yen.

the scoop

Capsule hotels are a unique form of accommodation available mostly in the busy entertainment areas in Tokyo. Capsules measuring 1m by 2m by 1m, equipped with light, ventilation fan, alarm clock and TV are stacked on one another. At approximately 3,000 yen per night, capsule hotels are very cheap and affordable. However, if you are a light sleeper, you may not get any sleep at all as the capsules tend to have poor sound insulation. Some of these hotels are for men only, and some have separate floors for men and women.

check out

It's time to go.

What time do we have to check out?	チェックアウトは何時ですか？ *chekku auto wa nanji desu ka*
May I have my bill, please?	清算お願いします。 *seisan onegai shimasu*
I think there's a mistake in this bill.	明細書に間違いがあるようなのですが。 *meisai sho ni machigai ga aruyoo nanodesuga*
I've taken ... from the mini-bar.	ミニバーから...を取りました。 *minibaa kara ... o torimashita* *You lush.*

5 FOOD

where to eat

What are ya in the mood for?

Let's go to …	…に行きましょう。
	… ni ikimashoo
a buffet.	ビュッフェ
	byuffe
a cafe.	カフェ
	kafe
a cafeteria.	カフェテリア
	kafeteria
a fast-food joint.	ファーストフード店
	faasuto-fuudo ten
a pizzeria.	ピザ屋
	piza-ya
a restaurant.	レストラン
	resutoran
a little eating place.	食堂
	shokudoo
a sushi restaurant.	寿司屋
	sushi-ya
a soba noodle shop.	蕎麦屋
	soba-ya
a family restaurant (diner).	ファミリーレストラン
	famirii resutoran
a BBQ restaurant.	焼肉屋
	yakiniku-ya

Now that you know where to eat, you'd better learn when to eat.

Breakfast can start as early as 6 am, but a more typical timing is between 7 to 8 am. Most restaurants and eateries will switch to the lunch menu after 10 am.

Lunch is served from 11.30 am to 1.30 pm. Lunches are light and quick meals for most Japanese.

Dinner is served between 6 pm and 8 pm.

the Scoop

Dining in Japanese restaurants is known to be an expensive affair. If you don't see prices next to seafood dishes on the menu, it is because the prices of these items fluctuate according to their availability in the different seasons.

fast food

In a rush? Grab a quick bite to eat so you can keep sightseeing…

Is there a … restaurant nearby?	近くに...レストランはありますか？ *chikaku ni … resutoran wa arimasu ka*
cheap	安い *yasui*
Japanese	和食 *washoku*

vegetarian	ベジタリアン	*bejitarian*
Where can I find …?	…はどこにありますか？	*… wa doko ni arimasu ka?*
a burger stand	ハンバーガーショップ	*hanbaagaa shoppu*
a café	カフェ	*kafe*
a fast-food joint	ファーストフード店	*faasuto-fuudo ten*
a pizzeria	ピザ屋	*piza-ya*
noodle stand	立ち食いの店	*tachigui no mise*
I'd like …	…をください。	*… o kudasai*
a burger.	ハンバーガー	*hanbaagaa*
fries.	フライドポテト	*furaido-poteto*
a pizza.	ピザ	*piza*
a sandwich.	サンドイッチ	*sandoicchi*
It's to go.	持って帰ります。	*motte kaerimasu*
That's all, thanks.	それだけです。	*soredake desu*
Enjoy your meal!	どうぞお食事をお楽しみください!	*dozo oshokuji o otanoshimi kudasai*

If you think you see noodle shops everywhere you go; on every street, that's because noodles (ramen, soba & udon) are the traditional Japanese fast food! Other cheap and filling snacks include tako-yaki (octopus dumplings), tai-yaki (fish-shaped sweet waffles), and baked goods and sandwiches from local bakeries.

table manners

Go ahead, treat yourself. You deserve a meal at a swanky restaurant!

A table for two, please.	二人なんですが、テーブルはありますか？ *futari nandesuga teeburu wa arimasu ka*
Could we sit …?	….に座りたいのですが。 *… ni suwaritai nodesuga*
outside	外 *soto*
in a non-smoking area	禁煙席 *kin'enseki*
by the window	窓際 *madogiwa*
Where are the restrooms?	トイレはどこですか？ *toire wa doko desu ka*
Waiter! / Waitress!	ウェイター / ウェイトレス *weitaa / weitoresu*

May I know what is this?	これは何ですか？ *kore wa nan desu ka*
Could you tell me what …is?	…はどのようなものですか？ *… wa donoyoona mono desu ka*
What is special for today?	今日の特別メニューは何ですか？ *kyoo no tokubetsu menyuu wa nan desu ka*
Do you have any set meal?	セットミールはありますか？ *setto-miiru wa arimasu ka*
I would like to have a lunch box.	弁当をください。 *bento o kudasai*
What's in it?	何が入っていますか？ *nani ga haitte imasu ka*
Without …	…なしでお願いします。 *… nashi de onegaishimasu*
Can I have some wasabi and soya sauce?	わさびと醤油をいただけますか？ *wasabi to shoyu o itadakemasu ka*
May I have some …?	…をください。 *… o kudasai*
I can't eat food containing …	…が入った食べ物は食べられません。 *… ga haitta tabemono wa taberaremasen*
Do you have vegetarian meals?	ベジタリアン用のメニューはありますか？ *bejitarian yoo no menyuu wa arimasu ka*
I'm a vegan.	私は菜食主義者です。 *watashi wa saishoku shugisha desu*

1. Before tucking into a meal, the Japanese say "itadaki-masu" (which more or less means "let's eat"). After a meal, they say "gochiso-sama deshita" to show appreciation for the food and the effort put in to get the meal ready. When someone buys you a meal or offers you some food, it is absolutely necessary to say "gochiso-sama deshita" after you have had your meal or food.

2. When eating sushi, try using your hands, and not the chopsticks. Dip the top (the side with the fish or shellfish) into soy sauce and consume the sushi in a single bite. Make sure you find out your 'tolerance' level for wasabi before sending that sushi into your mouth!

3. Japanese soups, such as miso soup, should be sipped directly from the bowl. Don't ask for a spoon and look like a cultural misfit!

4. When you use chopsticks, don't wave them over your food indecisively, never spear your food with the chopsticks, and don't pass food back and forth with chopsticks.

complaints

Go ahead and make a big stink.

That's not what I ordered.

これは私が注文したものと違います。
kore wa watashi ga cyuumon shitamono towa chigaimasu

I asked for …	...を注文したのですが。 *… o cyuumon shita nodesuga*
The food is cold.	料理が冷たいのですが。 *ryoori ga tsumetai nodesuga*
This isn't clean.	これは汚いのですが。 *kore wa kitanai nodesuga*
How much longer will our food be?	料理がまだ来ません。あとどれくらいかかりますか？ *ryori ga mada kimasen. Ato dorekurai kakarimasu ka*
We can't wait any longer. We're leaving.	これ以上待てません。もう帰ります。 *koreijoo matemasen. Moo kaerimasu*
We have been waiting for a long time.	もう随分待っています。 *moo zuibun matte imasu*
We have a bus to catch. Can you do our order first?	バスに乗るので、急いでもらえませんか？ *basu ni norunode, isoide moraemasen ka*

good or gross?

Give the chef a compliment – or not.

It's…	これは… *kore wa …*
delicious.	おいしいです。 *oishii desu*
disgusting.	まずいです。 *mazui desu*
This dish tastes great.	この料理はとてもおいしいです。 *kono ryori wa totemo oishii desu*
You are a great cook.	お料理がとても上手ですね。 *oryori ga totemo joozu desune*

It's …	これは…
	kore wa …
foul.	まずいです。
	mazui desu
(super) good.	（とても）おいしいです。
	(totemo) oishii desu
gross.	ひどい味です。
	hidoi aji desu
vile.	おいしくないです。
	oishikunai desu
Sorry, I'm not used to the taste.	すみません、慣れない味です。
	sumimasen, narenai aji desu
It has a rather unique taste.	とても独特な味ですね。
	totemo dokutoku na aji desune

pay up

How much did that meal set you back?

The check, please.	お勘定お願いします。
	okanjoo onegaishimasu
We'd like to pay separately.	別々に支払います
	betsubetsu ni shiharaimasu
	Goin' Dutch?
It's all together, please.	一緒にお願いします。
	issho ni onegai shimas
I think there's a mistake in this check.	この請求書は間違っているようなのですが。
	kono seikyuusho wa machigatte iruyoo nanodesuga
What is this amount for?	この金額は何ですか？
	kono kingaku wa nandesu ka

I didn't have that. I had …	それは頼んでいません。頼んだのは...です。
	sore wa tanonde imasen. Tanondanowa … desu
Is service included?	サービス料は含まれていますか？
	saabisu ryoo wa fukumarete imasu ka
	Sometimes it is, sometimes it isn't—always best to ask.
Can I pay with this credit card?	このクレジットカードで支払うことはできますか？
	kono kurejitto kaado de shiharau kotowa dekimasu ka
I've forgotten my wallet.	財布を持ってくるのを忘れました。
	saifu o mottekuruno o wasuremashita
I don't have enough money.	お金が足りないのですが。
	okane ga tarinai nodesuga
Could I have a receipt?	レシートをください。
	reshiito o kudasai

FACT

Tipping is not necessary in Japan as most establishments have already included a 10-15% service charge in the bill.

breakfast

Whether you have it early or late , ask for…

I'd like (some) …	...をください。
	… o kudasai
bread.	パン
	pan
butter.	バター
	bataa

eggs.	卵
	tamago
jam.	ジャム
	jamu
juice.	ジュース
	jyuusu
milk.	ミルク
	miruku
rolls.	ロールパン
	roorupan
toast.	トースト
	toosuto

soup's on

Homemade and delicious – here are the top picks.

Miso soup	味噌汁
	misoshiru
Japanese clear soup	吸い物
	suimono
Clam soup	蛤の吸い物
	hamaguri no suimono
Pork (& vegetable) soup	豚肉（と野菜）のスープ
	buta-niku (to yasai) no suupu

seafood

The coastal areas of Japan are well-known for their fish and seafood. You've gotta try...

| Assorted sashimi | 刺身の盛り合わせ |
| | *sashimi no moriawase* |

Fried turban shell	サザエのつぼ焼き *sazae no tsuboyaki*
Grilled salmon / saury / horse mackerel	焼き鮭 / サンマ / アジ *yaki sake / sanma / aji*
Freshly-chopped horse mackerel	アジのたたき *aji no tataki*
Teriyaki yellowtail snapper / swordfish / sablefish /cuttlefish	ブリ / メカジキ / 銀鱈/ イカの照り焼き *buri / mekajiki / gindara / ika no teriyaki*
Raw pink shrimp	甘海老 *ama-ebi*

the scoop

Fugu (blow fish, or puffer fish) is a fish which contains deadly toxins in its internal organs. Great care and precision is required when preparing fugu dishes, otherwise the meal could be a fatal one. Despite the obvious risks, fugu dishes remain a prized item on special feasts in Japan.

sashimi

Raw deal.

I'd like some …	…をください。 *… o kudasai.*
pink shrimp	甘海老 *ama-ebi*
prawn	海老 *ebi*
octopus	蛸 *tako*

cuttlefish	イカ *ika*
tuna	マグロ *maguro*
fatty tuna	トロ *toro*
salmon	鮭 *sake*
horse mackerel	アジ *aji*
arch shell	赤貝をください *akagai o kudasai*
What do you recommend?	何がお勧めですか？ *nani ga osusume desu ka*
Any seasonal specials at the moment?	今の季節は何がおいしいですか？ *ima no kisetsu wa nani ga oishii desu ka*
I'm allergic to shellfish.	甲殻類にアレルギーがあります。 *kookakurui ni arerugii ga arimasu*
Wow! That is expensive!	うわー！高いですね！ *uwaa! Takai desune*
Wow! The wasabi is hot!	うわー！わさびが辛いです！ *uwaa! Wasabi ga karai desu*
The sashimi is delicious!	刺身がとてもおいしいです！ *sashimi ga totemo oishii desu*
Can I have another serving of the …?	…をお代わりしたいのですが。 *…o okawari shitai nodesuga*

you carnivore

A meat-eater's dream come true. Here are the must haves.

I'd like some …   …をください。
                                   … o kudasai

Shabu-shabu   しゃぶしゃぶ
                       shabu shabu

Matsusaka beef   松坂牛
                       matsuzaka-gyuu
                       top quality meat of domestically-
                       grown cattle

Sukiyaki   すき焼き
                       sukiyaki

Free-range chicken   地鶏
                       jidori

Pork cutlet   豚カツ
                       tonkatsu

herbivore

For something a little lighter, try these favorites.

山菜うどん
sansai udon
noodle with wild vegetables

里芋の煮っころがし
sato-imo no nikkorogashi
taro cooked with soy sauce and sugar

金平ごぼう
kinpira-goboo
burdock and carrot strips sauteed with soy sauce and sugar

筍御飯
takenoko gohan
mixed rice with bamboo shoot and other vegetables

the scoop

Seasonal fruits are regarded as desserts. A great variety of fruit is available all year round. But autumn is probably the best season for fruit lovers. Try Japanese persimmons, chestnuts, pears, grapes, oranges and apples.

dessert

End your meal with any one of these delicious sweets.

大福もち
daifuku-mochi
rice cake stuffed with red bean paste

どらやき
dora-yaki
pancakes stuffed with red bean paste

あんみつ
an-mitsu
colorful jelly with red beans and syrup

草もち
kusa-mochi
rice cakes made with herbs and stuffed with red bean paste

street fest

Cheap and good food.

What's this? / What do you call this?	これは何ですか？/ これは何というものですか？ *kore wa nan desu ka / kore wa nan to iu mono desu ka*

| How much is one drink / plate / piece? | 一杯 / 一皿 / 一ついくらですか？ |
| | *ippai / hitosara / hitotsu ikura desu ka* |

| Give me one drink / plate / piece. | 一杯 / 一皿 / 一つください。 |
| | *ippai / hitosara / hitotsu kudasai* |

How do you eat this? Can you show me?	これはどうやって食べるのですか？
	やって見せてくれませんか？
	kore wa dooyatte taberu nodesu ka
	Yatte misete kuremasen ka

| Can you give me a bag to put this in? | これを入れる袋をもらえますか？ |
| | *kore o ireru fukuro o moraemasu ka* |

yo! Look out for these yummy Japanese snacks, and try them out – "senbei" (rice crackers), "wagashi" (delicately-made, sweet rice cakes with red bean paste), "dorayaki" (pancake sandwiches filled with sweet red bean paste), and "dango" (flavored dumplings made with rice flour).

overeating

Did you just pig out?

| I'm full. | おなかが一杯です。 |
| | *onaka ga ippai desu* |

| I ate too much. | 食べ過ぎました。 |
| | *tabesugi mashita* |

| I'm overstuffed. | おなかパンパンです。 |
| | *onaka panpan desus* |

what to drink

When you need to detox, ask for…

I'd like a …　　　　　　　…をください。
　　　　　　　　　　　　… o kudasai

(hot) chocolate.　　　　（ホット）チョコレート
　　　　　　　　　　　　(hotto) chokoreeto

coke.　　　　　　　　　コーラ
　　　　　　　　　　　　koora

juice.　　　　　　　　　ジュース
　　　　　　　　　　　　jyuusu

apple　　　　　　　　　りんご
　　　　　　　　　　　　ringo

grapefruit　　　　　　　グレープフルーツ
　　　　　　　　　　　　gureepu-furuutsu

orange　　　　　　　　　オレンジ
　　　　　　　　　　　　orenji

mineral water.　　　　　ミネラルウォーター
　　　　　　　　　　　　mineraru-wootaa

carbonated　　　　　　　炭酸
　　　　　　　　　　　　tansan

non-carbonated　　　　　炭酸なしの
　　　　　　　　　　　　tansan nashi no

coffee culture

Get your daily dose of caffeine.

I'd like a cup of tea / coffee.　　　紅茶 / コーヒーをください。
koocya / koohii o kudasai

A black coffee.　　　ブラックコーヒー
burakku-koohii

An espresso.　　　エスプレッソ
esupuresso

Coffee with milk, please.　　　ミルク入りのコーヒーをお願いします。
miruku iri no koohii o onegaishimasu

54

beer

Ready for a buzz?

Do you have ... beer? ...ビールはありますか？
... biiru wa arimasu ka

bottled 瓶
bin

draft 生
nama

A...beer, please. ...ビールをお願いします。
... biiru o onegaishimasu

Light ライト
raito

red レッド
reddo

white ホワイト
howaito

the scoop

The Japanese love their beer! Try local brands like Kirin,
Sapporo or Asahi. If you feel adventurous, try "Yebisu",
Japanese black beer, brewed by Sapporo.

drink up

There's no faster way to get a party started.

Do you want …?	…いかがですか？
	… ikagadesu ka
an aperitif	食前酒（を）
	shokuzenshu (o)
wine	ワイン（を）
	wain (o)
a glass of red wine	赤ワインを一杯
	aka-wain o ippai
a shot	一杯
	ippai
a gin and tonic	ジントニック（を）
	jintonikku (o)
a screwdriver	スクリュードライバー（を）
	sukuryuudoraibaa (o)

FACT

Tipping is not necessary in Japan as most establishments have already included a 10-15% service charge in the bill.

wine

Go ahead and order a glass – or bottle – of the best.

May I see the wine list, please?	ワインリストを見せてください。 *wain risuto o misete kudasai*
Can you recommend a wine?	どのワインがおすすめですか？ *dono wain ga osusume desu ka*
I'd like … of …	…を...でください。 *… o … de kudasai*
a bottle	ボトル *botoru*
a carafe	カラフ *karafu*
a glass	グラス *gurasu*

> **yo!** Sake is also known as "Nihonshu" (Japanese wine). It has about 15% alcohol content and can be served hot ("atsukan") or cold ("hiya"). Shochu is made from rice, yam, grain and potato and has about 25% alcohol content. Good quality shochu is best enjoyed on the rocks. But nowadays, shochu is sometimes mixed with juice or soda and sold as "chuhai" (wine coolers). Chuhai is very popular wih the younger crowd. Another drink that is gaining popularity is a cheaper and milder "beer-like" beverage called "Happoshu".

Make friends at a bar.

- 一杯おごらせてください。
  ippai ogorasete kudasai.
  Can I buy you a drink?

- いいんですか？　ありがとう。
  iindesu ka? Arigatoo.
  Sure, why not.

cheers

Before you drink, make a toast.

Let's celebrate!	乾杯!
	kanpai
Let's cheer!	乾杯!
	kanpai
Cheers!	乾杯!
	kanpai

"Kanpai!" After a hard day's work, Japanese white-collar workers congregate at the "izakaya" (local bistro) to unwind and de-stress. Office drinking parties (called "nomikai") are part-and-parcel of social life at work. During the "nomikai", it is acceptable to drink to your heart's content, and get drunk. Frank and emotional exchanges between co-workers are not taken seriously, and ignored or forgotten after the event. "Kanpai" literally means "bottoms up", so get ready to drink up!

hangover

Drank too much? Not feeling well?

I like to drink.	私は飲むのが好きです。 *watashi wa nomunoga suki desu*
I'm tipsy!	酔っ払ったみたいです！ *yopparatta mitai desu*
I've had one drink too many.	飲みすぎました。 *nomisugi mashita*
I'm hung over.	二日酔いです。 *futsukayoi desu*

FACT The minimum drinking age in Japan is 20. Drinking outdoors in the open is not frowned upon; unless you are an obstruction to traffic or become a nuisance to others. In fact, the Japanese love to sit in the open, under trees, drinking, having a picnic and singing while admiring the cherry-blossoms in March and April each year.

7 HAVIN' FUN

beach bum

Grab your shades and get some sun.

Is it a nude beach?	ここはヌーディストビーチ ですか？ *koko wa nuudisuto biichi desu ka*
Is there a swimming pool here?	ここにプールはありますか？ *koko ni puuru wa arimasu ka*
Is it safe to swim / dive here?	ここで泳ぐ / 潜るのは安全 ですか？ *koko de oyogu / moguru nowa anzen desu ka*
Is there a lifeguard?	監視員はいますか？ *kanshi-in wa imasu ka* *What you really want to know is: Is the lifeguard hot?!*
I want to rent …	…を借りたいのですが。 *… o karitai nodesuga*
a deck chair.	デッキチェア *dekki-chea*
a jet ski.	ジェットスキー *jetto-sukii*
a motorboat.	モーターボート *mootaa booto*
a surfboard.	サーフボード *saafuboodo*
an umbrella.	パラソル *parasoru*
waterskis.	水上スキー *suijoo-sukii*

surfing it up

Ride the big wave.

Which beach is the best for surfing around here?	この辺でサーフィンに最適な ビーチはどこですか？ *kono hen de saafin ni saiteki na biichi wa doko desu ka*
How can I get there?	そこまでの行き方を教えて ください。 *sokomadeno ikikata o oshiete kudasai*
How much is it to rent a surf board for ...?	サーフボードのレンタル料は … につきいくらですか *saafuboodo no rentaru-ryo wa … nitsuki ikura desu ka*
an hour	1時間 *ichi-jikan*
half a day	半日 *han-nichi*
a full day	1日 *ichi-nichi*
That's a really big wave!	とても大きな波ですね！ *totemo ookina nami desune*
Are there any dangerous <u>spots</u> / <u>areas</u> around here?	この辺に危険な<u>スポット</u> / <u>場所</u>は ありますか？ *kono hen ni kiken na supotto / basho wa arimasu ka*
You surf very well!	サーフィンがとても上手ですね！ *saafin ga totemo joozu desune*

the scoop

There are fantastic surfing spots all over Japan. Around Tokyo, there is (1) the Kujukuri Beach Line (in Chiba), (2) Shonan (in Kanagawa), and (3) Hazaki (in Ibaraki). In Chubu (central Honshu), there's Tahara and Toyohashi (in Aichi). In Shikoku, there's Ikumi beach (in Kochi), and southern Tokushima prefecture. In Kyushu, there's Okuragahama and Kanegahama in Miyagi prefecture.

party time

Let the Japanese show you how to have a good time.

What's there to do at night?	夜はどんなことができますか？ *yoru wa don'nakotoga dekimasu ka*
Let's hang out tonight.	今夜、一緒に遊びに行きましょう。 *kon'ya, issho ni asobi ni ikimashoo*

the scoop

In Tokyo, don't miss Roppongi, Shinjuku and Shibuya if you want to soak in the nightlife of metropolitan Japan. In Kyoto, go to Pontocho and the Kiyamachi district to party into the night. If you are in Osaka, don't forget Dotomburi.

Let's go to …	一緒に...に行きましょう。 *issho ni … ni ikimashoo*
the movies.	映画 *eiga*
the theater.	映画館 *eiga-kan*
a concert.	コンサート *konsaato*
Can you recommend a …?	おすすめの...はありますか？ *osusumeno … wa arimasu ka*
Is there … in town?	町には...がありますか？ *machi niwa … ga arimasu ka*
a bar	バー *baa*
a casino	カジノ *kajino*
a dance club	ダンスクラブ *dansu-kurabu*
a gay club	ゲイクラブ *gei-kurabu*
a nightclub	ナイトクラブ *naito-kurabu*
What type of music do they play?	どんな音楽を流していますか？ *don'na ongaku o nagashite imasu ka*
How do I get there?	そこまでの行き方を教えてください。 *sokomadeno ikikata o oshiete kudasai*

smoke

Whether you'd like to light up or want to share your distaste of smoking with those around you, here's the language you need.

Do you smoke?	煙草を吸いますか？	*tabako o suimasu ka*
Want to have a smoke?	一服しませんか？	*ippuku shimasen ka*
Do you have a cigarette?	煙草を持っていますか？	*tabako o motte imasu ka*

FACT

Smoking is prohibited in public spaces such as stations, department stores, trains, buses, and taxis. There are however, designated smoking areas. Many restaurants have smoking and non-smoking sections. Bars and clubs are still not entirely smoke-free.

spa

You need complete relaxation.

I'd like ...	...をお願いします。	*... o onegaishimasu*
a facial.	フェイシャル	*feisharu*
a manicure.	マニキュア	*manikyua*
a massage.	マッサージ	*massaaji*
a pedicure.	ペディキュア	*pedikyua*

a bikini wax.	ビキニワックス
	bikini-wakkusu
an eyebrow wax.	眉ワックス
	mayu-wakkusu

hot spring

Soak yourself and relax.

Do you have common areas for men and women?	混浴はありますか？
	kon'yoku wa arimasu ka
Where is the men's/women's area?	男湯 / 女湯はどこですか？
	otoko-yu / On'na-yu wa doko desu ka
Do I have to take off all my clothes?	着ているものを全部脱がないといけないのですか？
	kiteiru-mono o zenbu nuganaito ikenai nodesu ka
This is my first time at a hot spring.	温泉は初めてです。
	onsen wa hajimete desu
The water is too hot / cold!	とても熱い / 冷たいです！
	totemo atsui / tsumetai desu
I feel faint. I need to take a break.	のぼせてしまいました。少し休憩します。
	nobosete shimaimashita. Sukoshi kyuukei shimasu

body alterations

Blend in with the locals.

Did you have plastic surgery?	整形手術を受けたことがありますか？ *seikei-shujutsu o uketakoto ga arimasu ka?*
I had …	…を受けました。 *… o ukemashita*
a boob job.	豊胸手術 *hookyoo-shujutsu*
a nose job.	鼻の整形手術 *hana no seikei-shujutsu*
a tummy tuck.	腹部の整形手術 *fukubu no seikei-shujutsu*
I had my lips enhanced.	口の整形手術を受けました。 *kuchi no seikei-shujutsu o ukemashita*
He / She got a tattoo.	彼 / 彼女は刺青をしています。 *kare / kanojo wa irezumi o shiteimasu*
He / She has a / an …piercing.	彼 / 彼女は…にピアスをしています。 *kare / kanojo wa … ni piasu o shiteimasu*
belly button	臍 *heso*
eyebrow	眉 *mayu*
nipple	乳首 *chikubi*
nose	鼻 *hana*

the sights

Now that you're looking good, see and be seen.

Where's the tourist information office?	観光案内所はどこですか？ *kankooan'naijo wa doko desu ka*
Can you recommend a sightseeing tour?	おすすめの観光ツアーはありますか？ *osusume no kankoo tsuaa wa arimasu ka*
Are there any trips to …?	…へのツアーはありますか？ *…eno tsuaa wa arimasu ka*
What time does the tour start?	ツアーの出発は何時ですか？ *tsuaa no shupattsu wa nanji desu ka*
How much does the tour cost?	ツアーの料金はいくらですか？ *tsuaa no ryokin wa ikura desu ka*
What time do we get back?	戻るのは何時になりますか？ *modoru nowa nanji ni narimasu ka*
Is there an English-speaking guide?	英語を話すガイドはいますか？ *eigo o hanasu gaido wa imasu ka*
Can we stop here …?	ここでちょっと停まって...ことはできますか？ *kokode chotto tomatte … kotowa deki masu ka*
to buy souvenirs	土産を買う *miyage o kau*
to use the restrooms	トイレに行く *toire ni iku*
to take photographs	写真を撮る *shashin o toru* Capture the memory.

Would you take a photo of us?	私たちの写真を撮ってくれませんか？
	watashi-tachi no shashin o totte kure masen ka
	Ask a cute Japanese guy or girl!
Where is …?	…はどこですか？
	… wa doko desu ka
the art gallery	アートギャラリー
	aato gyararii
the botanical garden	植物園
	shokubutsuen
Where is …?	…はどこですか？
	… wa doko desu ka
the castle	城
	shiro
the cemetery	墓地
	bochi
the church	教会
	kyookai
the downtown area	繁華街
	hankagai
the market	市場
	ichiba
the (war) memorial	（戦争）記念碑
	(sensoo) kinenhi
the museum	博物館
	hakubutsukan
the old town	下町
	shitamachi
the palace	皇居
	kookyo
the shopping area	ショッピングエリア
	shoppingu eria

69

the tower	塔
	tou
the town hall	市役所
	shiyakusho
How much is the entrance fee?	入場料はいくらですか？
	nyuujoo-ryo wa ikura desu ka
Are there any discounts for students?	学生割引はありますか？
	gakusei waribiki wa arimasu ka

the scoop

Did you see something totally cool? Here are the top ten ways to say it.

Cool!	格好いい！
	kakkoo ii!
Very cool!	すごく格好いい！
	sugoku kakkoo ii!
Great!	素晴らしい！
	subarashii!
Great!	すごい！
	sugoi!
Killer!	しびれる！
	shibireru!
Nice!	素敵！
	suteki!
Perfect!	ばっちり！
	sacchiri!
Super!	最高！
	saikoo!

the scoop

| Super! | 素敵!
suteki! |
| Sweet! / Brilliant! | かわいい！/ 素晴らしい！
kawaii ! / subarashii! |

entertainment

In the mood for a little culture?

Do you have a program of events?	イベントのプログラムはありますか？ *ibento no puroguramu wa arimasu ka*
Can you recommend a good ...?	お勧めのいい...はありませんか？ *osusume no ii ... wa arimasen ka*
concert	コンサート *konsaato*
movie	映画 *eiga*
When does it start?	何時に始まりますか？ *nanji ni hajimarimasu ka*
Where can I get tickets?	どこでチケットを手に入れられますか？ *doko de chiketto o te ni ireraremasu ka*
How much are the seats?	席はいくらですか？ *seki wa ikura desu ka*

Do you have anything cheaper?	もう少し安いものはありませんか？
	moo sukoshi yasui monowa arimasen ka
Can I have a program?	プログラムをもらえますか？
	puroguramu o moraemasu ka

movies

Behind-the-scenes movie lingo…

My favorite movies are …	私の好きな映画は...です。
	watashi no sukina eiga wa … desu
comedies.	コメディ
	komedi
dramas.	ドラマもの
	dorama-mono
foreign films.	外国映画
	gaikoku-eiga
thrillers.	スリラー
	suriraa
psycho-thrillers.	サイコスリラー
	saiko-suriraa
What's playing at the movies?	映画館では何を上映していますか？
	eiga-kan dewa nani o jooei shiteimasu ka
Is the movie dubbed / subtitled?	映画は吹き替え / 字幕付きですか？
	eiga wa fukikae / jimaku-tsuki desu ka

music

Get into the groove – J POP

Do you like …?	…はお好きですか？
	… wa osukidesu ka

dance music	ダンスミュージック
	dansu myuujikku

hip-hop	ヒップホップ
	hippu hoppu

house (music)	ハウスミュージック
	hausu myuujikku

jazz	ジャズ
	jazu

pop (music)	ポップミュージック
	poppu myuujikku

rap	ラップ
	rappu

reggae	レゲエ
	regee

rock and roll	ロックンロール
	rokkunrooru

techno	テクノ
	tekuno

I really like …	…が大好きです。
	… ga daisuki desu

country.	カントリーミュージック
	kantorii myuujikku

folk.	フォークミュージック *fooku myuujikku*
soul.	ソウルミュージック *sooru myuujikku*
Which band is playing?	演奏しているのは何ていうバンド ですか？ *ensoo shiteirunowa nanteiu bando desu ka*
Are they popular?	彼らは人気がありますか？ *karera wa ninki ga arimasu ka*

yo! Can't live without your tunes? Make sure you have these.

a CD player		CDプレーヤー *CD pureeyaa*
a discman		ディスクマン *disukuman*
an MP3 player		MP3プレーヤー *MP3 pureeyaa*
an iPod™		iPod *iPod*
earphones		イヤホーン *iyahoon*
a stereo		ステレオ *sutereo*

yo! Countless "matsuri" (local festivals) are celebrated in Japan throughout the year.

Japanese New Year ("Shogatsu") (1st January)

This is the most celebrated holiday in Japan. Most Japanese take this opportunity to take a vacation, travel and have some fun. Be warned that most shops are closed during this time. Shinto shrines are the only places that are busy and bustling with activity.

Coming of Age Day (Seijin No Hi)

Young ladies who turn 20 that year will be dressed in traditional kimonos and visit Shinto shrines to pray for health and prosperity.

Valentine's Day

In Japan, women are the ones who buy gifts for men (usually chocolates) on this day. The men reciprocate a month later on "White Valentine's Day" (14th of March) when it is their turn to present chocolates to the ladies in their lives.

Hina Matsuri (Doll Festival)

Dolls are cast out to sea in a ritual which symbolizes the casting away of one's bad luck and misfortune (like poor health).

Cherry blossom (sakura) festival

A much-loved festival in Japan, it heralds the coming of spring, and sees the locals organizing drinking parties in the open under the sakura trees (sometimes until the wee hours in the morning!).

Shichi Go San (7-5-3) Festival

Boys aged 3 and 5, and girls aged 3 and 7 visit Shinto shrines for prayers. Most will be wearing traditional kimonos for the first time in their lives.

Hounen Festival (Fertility Festival)

The word 'hounen' means 'harvest'. The festival and its ceremonial proceedings are supposed to bless the participants with a bountiful harvest, prosperity and fertility. In the town of Komaki, Nagoya, the event involves a free flow of sake, stalls selling festive foods and souvenirs (mostly phallus-related), and the procession of a large 'fertility symbol' from one shrine to another.

sports

Get active.

Do you want to try …?	**…をやってみませんか？** *… o yatte mimasen ka*
Judo	**柔道** *Judo*
Karate	**空手** *Karate*
Kendo	**剣道** *Kendo*
Aikido	**合気道** *Aikido*
Yoga	**ヨガ** *Yoga*

FACT

Sumo is a traditional form of wrestling that's been around for at least 2,000 years! It became a professional sport in the early Edo period (1603-1867). Six tournaments each lasting 15 days are held each year. The January, May and September tournaments are held in Tokyo. While the March, July and November tournaments take place in Osaka, Nagoya and Fukuoka respectively.

I…	**私は…をします。** *watashi wa … o shimasu.*
cycle.	**サイクリング** *saikuringu*
jog.	**ジョギング** *jogingu*
rollerblade.	**ローラーブレード** *rooraabureedo*

skateboard.	スケートボード	
	sukeetoboodo	
surf.	サーフィン	
	saafin	
swim.	スイミング	
	suimingu	
Do you want to play …?	…をしませんか？	
	… o shimasen ka	
basketball	バスケットボール	
	basuketto booru	
soccer	サッカー	
	sakkaa	
tennis	テニス	
	tenisu	
volleyball	バレーボール	
	vareebooru	

baseball

You bet! A league of their own…

Hit it hard !	強く打て！	
	tsuyoku ute	
Get him !	アウトにしろ！	
	auto ni shiro	
Good catch !	ナイスキャッチ！	
	naisu kyacchi	
Fantastic play !	ナイスプレー！	
	naisu puree	
Double up !	ダブルスコアー！	
	daburu appu	

extreme sports

Take your game to the next level.

I want to go …	私は…をしてみたいです。 *watashi wa … o shitemitai desu*
skateboarding	スケートボード *sukeeto-boodo*
inline-skating	インラインスケート *inrain-sukeeto*
snowboarding	スノーボード *sunoo-boodo*
windsurfing	ウィンドサーフィン *uindo-saafin*
para-gliding	パラグライダー *paraguraidaa*

spectator sports

Prefer watching sports to actually playing them?

Is there a soccer game this Saturday?	今度の土曜日にサッカーの試合はありますか？ *kondo no doyoobi ni sakkaa no shiai wa arimasu ka*
Which teams are playing?	どのチームの試合ですか？ *dono chiimu no shiai desu ka*
Can you get me a ticket?	私にチケットを取ってくれませんか？ *watashi ni chiketto o totte kuremasen ka?*
What's the admission charge?	入場料はいくらですか？ *nyuujooryo wa ikura desu ka?*

soccer match

Show that you're true sports fans by screaming these.

Go! 行け！
ike

Let's go! さあ行け！
saa ike

Get them! やっつけろ！
yattsukero

Goal! ゴール！
gooru

We're the champions! 優勝だ！
yuushou da

insults

Don't forget that harassing the referee and the opponent is part of your job as a spectator.

The referee took a bribe! レフリーは賄賂でももらっているのか！
refurii wa wairo demo moratte irunoka!

Throw him out! 退場！
taijoo

Get out! 引っ込め！
hikkome

So predictable! つまらない！
tsumaranai

What were you doing!? 何やってんだ！？
nani yattenda

Where were you looking!? どこ見てんだ！？
doko mitenda

| You suck! | 最低だ！ |
| | *saitei da* |

| He sucks! | 彼は最低だ！ |
| | *kare wa saitei da* |

| @#&! this player! | くそ、あいつめ！ |
| | *kuso, aitsume* |

pachinko

It ain't a pin-ball or slot machine.

| Can you show me how to do it? | どうやるのかやって見せてくれませんか？ |
| | *dooyarunoka misete kuremasen ka* |

| Is this machine working? | この台は動いていますか？ |
| | *kono dai wa ugoite imasu ka* |

| Will you kindly tell me which machine is good? | どの台がいいか教えてくれませんか？ |
| | *dono dai ga iika oshiete kuremasen ka* |

| Yes! I have won! | やった！勝った！ |
| | *yatta! katta* |

| Oh no! I have lost all my balls! | しまった！玉がもうなくなった！ |
| | *shimatta! tama ga moo nakunatta* |

| What can I get with these balls? | このパチンコ玉で何が貰えるのですか？ |
| | *kono pachinko-dama de nani ga moraeru nodesu ka* |

the
SCOOP

Pachinko parlors can be found in every city in Japan. Players purchase a large number of little steel balls which are poured into the pachinko machine altogether at the same time. From a tray at the base, the steel balls are 'launched' in quick succession to the top of the machine. The balls then drop though an array of pins on their way down to the bottom. With some intervention and control from the player, the balls may fall into select slots which make the machine pay out more steel balls. Winnings in the form of balls are used to continue playing or exchanged for prizes.

FACT

Gambling is currently illegal in Japan. But... various forms of gaming and betting related activities are available. They include: the lottery, mahjong, bets on officially managed races (like horse, bicycle, motorboat, and motorcycle races) and the all too famous pachinko.

training

Don't let your body go just because you're on vacation.

Can I use …?	…を使ってもいいですか？ *… o tsukattemo iidesu ka*
the fitness bike	フィットネスバイク *fittonesu-baiku*
the rowing machine	ローイングマシーン *rooingu-mashiin*
the treadmill	トレッドミル *toreddo-miru*
I feel great.	最高の気分です。 *saikoo no kibun desu*
I'm in shape.	体調がいいです。 *Taichoo ga ii desu*
I'm dead tired.	すごく疲れました。 *Sugoku tsukare mashita*
I can't take it anymore.	もうこれ以上はできません。 *moo koreijoo wa dekimasen*
I'm sick of it.	もううんざりです。 *moo unzaridesu*

9 MAKIN' FRIENDS

small talk

Get a conversation goin'.

My name is …	私の名前は...です。 *Watashi no namae wa … desu* *A simple way to introduce yourself.*
What's your name?	あなたの名前は何ですか？ *Anata no namae wa nandesu ka*
Where are you from?	どこから来たのですか？ *Dokokara kita nodesu ka*
Whom are you with?	誰かと一緒ですか？ *Dareka to issho desu ka*
I'm on my own.	一人です。 *Hitori desu*
I'm with a friend.	友達と一緒です。 *Tomodachi to issho desu* *Oh, really?!*
I'm with my …	...と一緒です。 *… to issho desu*
boyfriend / girlfriend.	ボーイフレンド / ガールフレンド *booi-furendo / gaaru-furendo*
family.	家族 *kazoku*
parents.	両親 *ryoshin*
father / mother.	父 / 母 *chichi / haha*
brother / sister.	兄弟 / 姉妹 *kyoodai / shimai*

chitchat

These will help you keep his or her attention.

What do you do?	お仕事は何ですか？ *oshigoto wa nandesu ka*
What are you studying?	何を勉強しているのですか？ *nani o benkyo shiteiru nodesu ka*

I'm studying ...	私は...を勉強しています。 *watashi wa ... o benkyo shiteimasu*
the arts.	芸術 *geijutsu*
business.	ビジネス *bijinesu*
engineering.	工学 *koogaku*
sales.	販売 *hanbai*
science.	科学 *kagaku*

| What are your interests? | あなたの関心？
anata no kanshin |
| What are your hobbies? | 趣味は何ですか？
shumi wa nandesu ka |

makin' plans

Get together.

Are you free tonight?	今夜、お暇ですか？ *kon'ya ohima desu ka*
Can you come for a drink this evening?	今晩、飲みに行きませんか？ *konban nomi ni ikimasen ka*
Would you like to …?	一緒に…のはいかがですか？ *issho ni … nowa ikaga desu ka*
go dancing	踊りに行く *odori ni iku*
go out to eat	外食する *gaishoku suru*
go for a walk	散歩に行く *sanpo suru*
Can I bring a friend?	友達も連れて行っていいですか？ *tomodachi mo tsurete itte iidesu ka*
Where should we meet?	どこで会いましょうか？ *doko de aimashoo ka*

hangin' out

Get a little closer with these.

| Let me buy you a drink. | 一杯おごらせてください。
ippai ogorasete kudasai |
| What are you going to have? | 何にしますか？
nani ni shimasu ka |

Why are you laughing?	何がおかしいのですか？
	nani ga okashiinodesu ka
Is my Japanese that bad?	私の日本語はそんなにひどいですか？
	watashi no Nihon-go wa son'na ni hidoi desu ka
Should we go somewhere quieter?	もっと静かなところに行きませんか？
	motto shizukana tokoro ni ikimasen ka
	Such as...?
Thanks for the evening.	今晩はありがとうございました。
	konban wa arigatoo gozaimashita

If you ask a someone out, you are expected to pay the bill. That's the rule. A guy who asks to "go Dutch" will be labeled "stingy" — and that's a huge turn-off. Once you are in a long-term relationship, things are a little different, and going Dutch is completely natural and acceptable to most couples.

get a date

Looking to score? Try these.

Hi, how are you?	やあ、元気？
	yaa, genki
	It's simple—but a good way to break the ice.

Hello, I don't think we've met.	こんにちわ、お会いするのは初めてですね。 *kon'nichiwa, oaisurunowa hajimete desune* *If it's is your first visit to Japan, it's certainly the truth!*
Would you like to sit down?	お座りになりませんか？ *osuwari ni narimasen ka* *This works wonders in a bar or on the subway.*
Do you mind if I sit here?	ここに座ってもいいですか？ *koko ni suwattemo iidesu ka*
Can I be your friend?	友達になってくれませんか？ *tomodachi ni natte kuremasen ka*
Do you have a boyfriend / girlfriend?	ボーイフレンド / ガールフレンドはいますか？ *booi-furendo / gaaru-furendo wa imasu ka*
Can I be your boyfriend / girlfriend?	私と付き合ってくれませんか？ *watashi to tsukiatte kuremasen ka*
You are very pretty / handsome.	あなたはとても可愛い / ハンサムですね *anata wa totemo kawaii / hansamu desune*
Do you believe in love at first sight?	ひと目ぼれを信じますか？ *hitomebore o shinjimasu ka*
I am serious about you.	あなたのことを真剣に考えています。 *anata no koto o shinken ni kangaete imasu*
You are really sexy.	あなたはとてもセクシーですね。 *anata wa totemo sekushii desune* *The perfect informal come-on to use in a bar or club.*

Are you a model?	あなたはモデルですか？
	anata wa moderu desu ka
	You'd be surprised how well this one works.
You look great!	とても素敵ですね！
	totemo suteki desune
You have beautiful eyes.	とても美しい目をしていますね。
	totemo utsukushii me o shiteimasune

refusals

Not your type? Here are the best ways to reject someone.

Thanks, but I'm expecting someone.	今、人を待っているので。
	ima, hito o matteirunode
	Whether this is true or not, he or she will get the hint.
Leave me alone, please.	私にかまわないでください。
	watashi ni kamawanaide kudasai
	Polite and to to the point.
You are not my type.	あなたは私の好みではありません。
	anata wa watashi no konomi dewa arimasen
Get the heck out of here!	ここから出て行け！
	koko kara deteike
Go away!	あっちへ行って！
	acchi e itte
	It's brutal, but effective.

gay?

Looking for some alternative fun?

Are you gay?	あなたはゲイですか？ *anata wa gei desu ka*
Do you like men / women?	あなたは男性 / 女性が好き ですか？ *anata wa dansei / josei ga sukidesu ka*
Let's go to a gay bar.	ゲイバーに行きましょう。 *gei baa ni ikimashoo*
He's gay.	彼はゲイです。 *kare wa gei desu*
She's a lesbian.	彼女はレズです。 *kanojo wa rezu desu*
Get out of the closet!	正直にカミングアウトしたら？ *shoojiki ni kaminguauto shitara*

Japanese laws offer some legal protection for gay men and women; although prejudice from the general public still exists. Events such as the Tokyo Pride Parade, the LesBiGay March in Sapporo, and the International Lesbian and Gay Film and Video Festival play an important role in highlighting gay rights and related issues.

the scoop

dating

Found a Japanese lover? Here's how to tell your love story.

I made out with him.

彼とやりました。
kare to yarimashita

I'm going out with her.

彼女と付き合っています。
kanojo to tsukiatte imasu

I french-kissed him.

彼とフレンチキスをしました。
kare to furenchi-kisu o shimashita

We got naked.

二人とも裸になりました。
futari tomo hadaka ni narimashita

sex

A variety of ways to state the obvious…

We …	私たちは… *watashi-tachi wa…*
slept together.	一緒に寝ました。 *issho ni nemashita*
made love.	セックスしました。 *sekkusu shimashita*
@#&!ed.	セックスしました。 *sekkusu shimashita*

safe sex

Protection is a must, in any language.

I use …	私は...を使います。 *watashi wa … o tsukaimasu*
condoms.	コンドーム *kondoomu*
the pill.	ピル *piru*
a diaphragm.	ペッサリー *pessarii*
Do you have a condom?	コンドームを持っていますか？ *kondoomu o motte imasu ka*
Are you using contraceptives?	避妊していますか？ *hinin shiteimasu ka*
Have you been tested for HIV?	エイズのテストは受けて いますか？ *eizu no tesuto wa ukete imasu ka*

break up

The best ways to end your holiday fling…

It's over between us.

私たちはもうお終いです。
watashi-tachi wa moo oshimai desu
Be firm!

Let's just be friends.

ただの友達になりましょう。
tada no tomodachi ni narimashoo
Say this only if you mean it.

I'm breaking up with you.

あなたと別れたいのです。
anata to wakaretainodesu
End of story…

closure

Did he or she dump you? Here are the nastiest things you can call your ex.

He is a scumbag.

嫌な奴！
iyana yatsu

He is a …

彼は...ね。
kare wa … ne

pathetic guy.

哀れな男
aware na otoko

loser.

ダメ男
dame otoko

She is a ...

彼女は...だ。
kanojo wa ... da

slut.

尻軽女
shirigaru on'na

bitch.

あばずれ
abazure

where to shop

Grab your wallet and go!

Are we going shopping?	ショッピングに行きましょうか？ *shoppingu ni ikimashoo ka*
Do you want to go window shopping?	ウィンドウショッピングに行きませんか？ *uindoo shoppingu ni ikimasen ka*
Where's the main mall?	大きなショッピングセンターはどこですか？ *ookina shoppingu sentaa wa doko desu ka*
I'm looking for …	…を探しているのですが。 *… o sagashite irunodesuga*
a boutique.	ブティック *butikku*
a department store.	デパート *depaato*
a flea market.	フリーマーケット *furii-maaketto*
a market.	市場 *ichiba*
an outlet store.	アウトレット店 *autoretto-ten*
a second-hand store.	リサイクルショップ *risaikuru-shoppu*
a vintage shop.	ヴィンテージショップ *vinteeji-shoppu*

Where can I find …	…はどこにありますか？ *… wa doko ni arimasu ka*
antiques	骨董品 *kottoohin*
cheap and trendy women's wear/men's wear?	安くて流行の婦人服 / 紳士服 *yasukute ryuukoo no fujin-fuku / shinshi-fuku*
handicraft	手工芸品 *shukoogeihin*
a night market	ナイトマーケット *naito-maaketto*
a street market	ストリートマーケット *sutoriito-maaketto*
When does the …open / close?	…は何時から / 何時までですか？ *…wa nanjikara / nanjimade desu ka*
Where's …?	…はどこですか？ *… wa doko desu ka*
the bookstore	本屋 *hon-ya*
the camera shop	カメラ店 *kamera-ten*

the health food store	健康食品店 *kenkooshokuhin-ten*
the jewelry store	宝石店 *hooseki-ten*
the liquor store	酒屋 *sakaya*
the market	市場 *ichiba*
the music store	音楽店 *ongaku-ten*
the newsstand	新聞売り場 *shinbun-uriba*
the pharmacy	薬局 *yakkyoku*
the shoe store	靴屋 *kutsu-ya*
the souvenir store	土産物屋 *miyagemono-ya*
the sports store	スポーツ用品店 *supootsu-yoohin-ten*

customer service

Ask the right question.

Where's ...?	...はどこですか？ *... wa doko desu ka?*
the escalator	エスカレーター *esukareetaa*
the store map	店内案内図 *ten'nai-an'naizu*

Where's ...?	...はどこですか？
	... wa doko desu ka
customer service	顧客サービス
	kokyakusaabisu
the fitting room	試着室
	shicyakushitsu
the lingerie department	下着売り場
	shitagi-uriba
the men's department	男性用売り場
	danseiyoo-uriba
the perfume / cosmetics department	香水 / 化粧品売り場
	koosui / keshoohin uriba
the register	レジ
	reji
the shoe department	靴売り場
	kutsu-uriba
the women's department	女性用売り場
	joseiyoo-uriba
Where can I find ...?	...はどこにありますか？
	... wa doko ni arimasu ka
boot-cut pants	ブーツカットのパンツ
	buutsukatto no pantsu
jeans	ジーンズ
	jiinzu
a leather jacket	革のジャケット
	kawa no jaketto
low-rise pants	ローライズのパンツ
	rooraizu no pantsu
a miniskirt	ミニスカート
	minisukaato

a polo shirt	ポロシャツ
	poroshatsu
I'm looking for …	…を探しているのですが。
	… o sagashiteiru nodesuga
a backpack.	バックパック
	bakkupakku
books / magazines.	本 / 雑誌
	hon / zasshi
CDs / DVDs.	CD / DVD
	CD / DVD

sales help

Here's how to ask that cute salesperson for assistance.

Can you help me?	手伝ってもらえますか？
	tetsudatte moraemasu ka
Can I try this on?	これを試してもいいですか？
	kore o tameshitemo iidesu ka
Where's the fitting room?	試着室はどこですか？
	shichakushitsu wa doko desu ka
Could you show me …?	…を見せてもらえますか？
	… o misete moraemasu ka
I'd like to buy …	…を買いたいのですが。
	… o kaitai nodesuga

yo! You may want to fill in the blanks above with any of these items.

baseball cap	**野球帽**	*yakyuu-boo*
bikini	**ビキニ**	*bikini*
bra	**ブラジャー**	*burajaa*
briefs	**ブリーフ**	*buriifu*
boxers	**ボクサーショーツ**	*bokusaa-shootsu*
coat	**コート**	*kooto*
denim jacket	**デニムジャケット**	*denimu-jaketto*
dress	**ドレス**	*doresu*
halter top, tank top	**ホルタートップ、タンクトップ**	*horutaatoppu, tankutoppu*
jeans	**ジーンズ**	*jiinzu*
messenger bag	**メッセンジャーバッグ**	*messenjaa-baggu*
shirt	**シャツ**	*shatsu*
shoes	**靴**	*kutsu*
shorts	**ショートパンツ**	*shooto-pantsu*

skirt	スカート
	sukaato
socks	ソックス
	sokkusu
sunglasses	サングラス
	sangurasu
swim trunks	水泳パンツ
	suiei-pantsu
thong	T バック
	T-baggu
tight T-shirt	タイトなTシャツ
	taito na t-shatsu

yo! Looking for something in a particular color? Ask for it in…

beige	ベージュ	orange	オレンジ
	beijyu		*orenji*
black	黒	pink	ピンク
	kuro		*pinku*
blue	青	purple	紫
	ao		*murasaki*
brown	茶色	red	赤
	chairo		*aka*
gray	灰色	white	白
	haiiro		*shiro*
green	緑	yellow	黄色
	midori		*kiiro*

at the register

Looking to part with your hard-earned dough? Here's the lingo you need to make your purchase.

How much?	いくらですか？ *ikura desu ka*
Where do I pay?	どこで払えばいいですか？ *doko de haraeba iidesu ka*
Do you accept travelers checks?	トラベラーズチェックは使えますか？ *toraberaazu chekku wa tsukaemasu ka*
Sorry, I don't have enough money.	ごめんなさい、お金が足りません。 *gomen'nasai, okane ga tarimasen*
Could I have a receipt please?	レシートをいただけますか？ *reshiito o itadakemasu ka*
I think you've given me the wrong change.	お釣りが間違っているみたいなのですが。 *otsuri ga machigatte irumitai nanodesuga*

bargains

Put your negotiating skills to use.

Is this on sale?	これはセール品ですか？ *kore wa seeru-hin desu ka*
That's too expensive.	高すぎます。 *takasugimasu*
It's pricey.	高いですね。 *takaidesune*
Will you lower the price?	値引きしてもらえませんか？ *nebiki shitemoraemasen ka*
Can you give me a discount?	割引してもらえませんか？ *waribiki shitemoraemasen ka*

Do you have anything cheaper?	他にもう少し安いものはありませんか？
	hoka ni moosukoshi yasuimono wa arimasen ka
I'll think about it.	もう少し考えます。
	moo sukoshi kangaemasu

the Scoop

If you are a bargain hunter, look out for the "end of summer" and "end of winter" sales. But take note that some sale events may require invitation cards from the shop or department store.

yo! Shopping in Japan can be expensive, but... there are some stores where you can find good bargains. Check out the 100-yen shops, flea markets, outlet malls, and specialty discount stores. The larger outlet malls are located in Makuhari (Chiba prefecture), Tama city (Tokyo suburb), Iruma city (Saitama prefecture), Yokohama (Kanagawa prefecture), Osaka and Kobe city.

problems

Is there something wrong with your purchase?

This doesn't work.	これは壊れています。
	kore wa kowarete imasu
Can you exchange this, please?	交換してもらえませんか？
	kookan shite moraemasen ka

I'd like a refund.	返金して欲しいのですが。
	henkin shite hoshii nodesuga
Here's the receipt.	これがレシートです。
	kore ga reshiito desu
I don't have the receipt.	レシートがありません。
	reshiito ga arimasen

FACT

Shopping in Japan may be fun, but who said it was easy? If you are not happy with your purchase, few stores will give you your money back --except when there is an obvious defect in the product. Some shops may be able to exchange your purchase with another product if your purchase has not been opened, used or worn. Exchange policies varies from store to store; do check with the shop before you make payment.

at the drugstore

Not feeling well? Here's some help.

Where's the nearest (all-night) pharmacy?	最寄の (終夜営業の) 薬局はどこですか？
	moyori no (shuuyaeigyou) no yakkyoku wa doko desu ka
Can you fill this prescription for me?	この処方せんの薬を下さい。
	kono shohoo sen no kusuri o kudasai
How much should I take?	1回の服用量はどれくらいですか？
	ikkai no hukuyoo-ryoo wa dorekurai desu ka
How often should I take it?	1日に何回服用するのでしょうか？
	ichi-nichi ni nankai hukuyoo surunode shoo ka
Are there any side effects?	副作用はありますか？
	fukusayoo wa arimasu ka

What would you recommend for ...?	...にはどれがいいですか？ *... niwa dore ga iidesu ka*
a cold	風邪 *kaze*
a cough	咳 *seki*
diarrhea	下痢 *geri*
a hangover	二日酔い *futsuka-yoi*
hay fever	花粉症 *kafunsho*
insect bites	虫さされ *mushi-sasare*
a sore throat	喉の痛み *nodo no itami*
sunburn	日焼け *hiyake*
motion sickness	乗り物酔い *norimono yoi*
an upset stomach	胃の不調 *i no fucho*
Can I get it without a prescription?	処方せんなしで買えますか？ *shohoosen nashi de kaemasu ka*
Can I have ...?	...をください。 *... o kudasai*
antiseptic cream	殺菌クリーム *sakkin kuriimu*
aspirin	アスピリン *asupirin*
bandages	包帯 *hootai*

| condoms | コンドーム |
| | *kondoomu* |

| bug repellent | 虫除け |
| | *mushiyoke* |

| painkillers | 痛み止め |
| | *itamidome* |

| vitamins | ビタミン剤 |
| | *bitaminzai* |

FACT

Most retail pharmacies and drug stores are open by 9am and close at 6pm. However, there are some that stay open till late. Apart from these drug stores, convenience stores such as Lawson or 7-11 also stock toiletries, bandages, lozenges and some medication.

toiletries

Forgot to pack something?

| I'd like ... | | ...が欲しいのですが。 |
| | | *... ga hoshii nodesuga* |

| aftershave. | | アフターシェーブ |
| | | *afutaasheebu* |

| conditioner. | | コンディショナー |
| | | *kondishonaa* |

| deodorant. | | デオドラント |
| | | *deodoranto* |

| moisturizing cream. | | モイスチャークリーム |
| | | *moisuchaa-kuriimu* |

| razor blades. | | かみそりの刃 |
| | | *kamisori no ha* |

| sanitary napkins. | | 生理用ナプキン |
| | | *seiriyoo-napukin* |

shampoo.		シャンプー *shanpuu*
soap.		石鹸 *sekken*
sun block.		日焼け止め *hiyakedome*
suntan lotion.		日焼けローション *hiyakerooshon*
tampons.		タンポン *tanpon*
tissues.		ティッシュペーパー *tisshu-peepaa*
toilet paper.		トイレットペーパー *toiretto-peepaa*
toothpaste.		歯磨き粉 *hamigakiko*

make-up

Ladies, get all dolled up.

I need some …	…が欲しいのですが。 *… ga hoshii nodesuga*
blush.	頬紅 *hoobeni*
eyeliner.	アイライナー *airainaa*
eye shadow.	アイシャドウ *aishadoo*
foundation.	ファンデーション *fandeeshon*
lipgloss / lipstick.	リップグロス / 口紅 *rippugurosu / kuchibeni*

mascara.	マスカラ
	masukara
powder.	フェイスパウダー
	feisu-paudaa

camera shop

Admit it, you're a tourist. You'll need these.

I'm looking for a disposable camera.	使い捨てカメラを探しているの ですが。
	tsukaisute kamera o sagashite iru nodesuga
Do you sell ... for digital cameras?	デジタルカメラ用の...は売って いますか？
	dejitaru kamera yoo no ... wa utte imasu ka
memory cards	メモリカード
	memori-caado
batteries	電池
	denchi
When will the photos be ready?	写真はいつできますか？
	shashin wa itsu dekimasu ka

the scoop

Japan is heaven for those into high-tech gizmos. Akihabara in Tokyo is the place to check out for all things high-tech. Walking through this digital town is like taking a stroll into the future and seeing what it has to offer. Den Den Town is the Akihabara of Osaka. It's famous for its extensive mix of consumer electronics and computer stores.

internet café

Stay in touch with friends and family at home.

Is there an internet café near here?	この近くにインターネットカフェはありますか？ *kono chikaku ni intaa'netto-kafe wa arimasu ka*
Can I access the internet here?	ここでインターネットにアクセスすることはできますか？ *koko de intaa'netto ni akusesu surukoto wa dekimasu ka*
What are the charges per hour?	1時間につきいくらですか？ *ichi-jikan ni tsuki ikura desu ka*
How do I log on?	ログオンはどうやるのでしょうか？ *rogu-on wa dooyaru nodeshoo ka*
I'd like to send a message by e-mail.	メールでメッセージを送りたいのですが。 *meeru de messeeji o okuritai nodesuga*
What's your e-mail address?	あなたのメールアドレスを教えてください。 *anata no meeru-adoresu o oshiete kudasai*

yo! The internet cafe is sometimes called "manga kissa" in Japan. There are approximately 4,000 such cafes nationwide. Internet cafes in Japan are not just about internet connection, most are well-stocked with comics, books and magazines. Since most cafes are open 24 hours, they are equipped with comfortable sofas, and some even have shower facilities. Soft drinks are usually offered free and the usage fee of a semi-private internet booth is around 400 yen per hour.

According to social surveys, there is a growing number of "Net cafe refugees" (people who have virtually made the Net café their home) in Japan and about 80% of them are men. Some of these "refugees" are simply addicted to the internet, others have been laid off and are killing time at the Net cafés to hide the fact that they are jobless from their families!

Check out …	**…を見て！** *… o mite!*
this cool computer.	**この格好いいコンピューター** *kono kakkoii konpyuutaa*
this cool laptop.	**この格好いいラップトップコンピューター** *kono kakkoii rappu-toppu konpyuutaa*
this cool mouse.	**この格好いいマウス** *kono kakkoii mausu*
Turn it on.	**スイッチを入れてください。** *suicchi o irete kudasai.*
Click here!	**ここをクリックしてください！** *koko o kurikku shite kudasai.*
I'm going to …	**…します。** *… shimasu*
go online.	**インターネットに接続** *intaa'netto ni setsuzoku*
send an e-mail.	**メールを送信** *meeru o sooshin*
You need to <u>logout</u> / <u>reboot</u>.	<u>**ログアウト**</u> / <u>**再起動**</u>**する必要があります。** *<u>rogu-auto</u> / <u>saikidoo</u> suru hitsuyoo ga arimasu*
My computer crashed.	**私のコンピューターが故障しました。** *watashi no konpyuutaa ga koshoo shimashita*

1

laptop

Brought your own laptop? You might need these questions.

Does this hotel / café have Wi-Fi®?	このホテル / カフェではWi-Fi は使えますか？ *kono hoteru / kafe de Wi-Fi wa tsukae-masu ka*
Where is the closest hotspot?	最寄りのホットスポットはどこ ですか？ *moyori no hottosupotto wa doko desu ka*
Is there a connection fee?	接続料はかかりますか？ *setsuzokuryo wa kakarimasu ka*
Do I have to register?	登録が必要ですか？ *tooroku ga hitsuyoo desu ka*
What's your favorite …	あなたのお気に入りの...は何 ですか？ *anata no okiniiri no … wa nandesu ka*
chatroom	チャットルーム *cyattoruumu*
webpage	ホームページ *hoomupeeji*
website	ウェブサイト *webusaito*
Can you …	….できますか？ *… dekimasu ka?*
IM someone	IMを送ることは *IM o okurukoto wa*
send me an e-mail	私にメールを送ることは *watashi ni meeru o okurukoto wa*
scroll <u>up</u> / <u>down</u>	スクロール<u>アップ</u>／<u>ダウン</u>は *sukurooru appu / daun wa*

phone call

From public to private, the language you need to make your call.

I'd like a phonecard.	テレホンカードが欲しいのですが。 *terefonkaado ga hoshii nodesuga*
I need to make a phone call.	電話をかける必要があるのですが。 *denwa o kakeru hitsuyoo ga aru nodesuga*
Can I …?	…いいですか？ *… iidesu ka*
get your number	あなたの電話番号を聞いても *anata no denwa-bangoo o kiitemo*
call you	あなたに電話しても *anata ni denwa shitemo*
make a call	電話をかけても *denwa o kaketemo*
I'll give you a call.	私から電話します。 *watashi kara denwa shimasu*
Here's my number.	これが私の電話番号です。 *kore ga watashi no denwa-bangoo desu*
Call me.	私に電話してください。 *watashi ni denwa shitekudasai*
Where's the nearest phone booth?	最寄の電話ボックスはどこですか？ *moyori no denwa-bokkusu wa doko desu ka*
May I use your phone?	電話を借してもらえませんか？ *denwa o kashite moraemasen ka*
It's an emergency.	緊急です。 *kinkyuu desu*

What's the number for Information?	番号案内は何番ですか？ *bangoo-an'nai wa nanban desu ka*
I'd like to call collect.	コレクトコールをかけたいのですが。 *korekutokooru o kaketai nodesuga*
Hello?	もしもし？ *moshi moshi*
Yes.	はい。 *hai*
It's …	…です。 *… desu*
It's me!	私です！ *watashi desu*
Could I speak with …?	… (さん) はいらっしゃいますか？ *… (san) wa irasshaimasu ka*
I'd like to speak to …	… （さん）はいますか？ *… (san) wa imasuka*
Can I leave a message?	伝言をお願いできますか？ *dengon o onegai dekimasu ka*
Hold on, please.	お待ちください。 *omachi kudasai*
When will he / she be back?	いつお戻りになりますか？ *itsu omodori ni narimasu ka*
Will you tell him / her that I called?	私から電話があったと伝えてもらえますか？ *watashi kara denwa ga atta to tsutaete moraemasu ka*
My name is …	私の名前は...です。 *watashi no namae wa … desu*

FACT

Public phones come in a variety of colors, shapes and sizes. There are different phones for domestic and international calls. Regular green payphones are for domestic calls only. To make a direct overseas call, use gray payphones with an international and domestic telephone sign, or tall green phones with gold faces. These phones are not common but they can be found at airports, some hotels, and other key facilities.

Direct overseas calls can be made by dialing an access number (like 001, 0033, or 0041), and then the country code, area code and telephone number. If you need assistance from an operator, dial 0051. While many phones do take coins, some only take specific phone cards.

Domestic calls cost 10 yen for the first three minutes, and 10 yen for each additional 80 seconds thereafter. International calls range from 30 yen to 360 yen for three minutes depending on where are you are calling. Most coin phones accept 10 and 100-yen coins. Phone cards come in 500, 1,000, 3,000, and 5,000 yen denominations. Phone cards can be bought from public vending machines and some retail stores. Look for a sign depicting a phone super-imposed over a card held in hand.

bye!

End that phone conversation with class.

I'll be in touch.	また連絡します。 *mata renraku shimasu*
Good-bye.	さようなら。 *sayoonara*
Gotta go.	もう行かなくちゃ。 *moo ikanakucha*

Later.	またね。
	matane
Love you.	愛しています。
	aishitemasu
Let's talk later.	また後で話しましょう。
	mata ato de hanashimashoo

snail mail

Mail your stuff.

Where is the post office?	郵便局はどこですか？
	yuubinkyoku wa doko desu ka
What time does the post office open / close?	郵便局は何時から / 何時まで ですか？
	yuubinkyoku wa nanji kara / nanji made desuka ka
A stamp for this postcard, please.	この絵葉書の切手をください。
	kono ehagaki no kitte o kudasai
What's the postage for a letter to …?	...までの手紙の郵便料金はいくら ですか？
	… madeno tegami no yuubin-ryookin wa ikura desu ka
I want to send this package …	この小包を...で送りたいの ですが。
	kono kozutsumi o … de okuritai nodesuga
by airmail.	航空便
	kookuu-bin
by express mail.	速達便
	sokutatsu-bin

DICTIONARY
Japanese ▸ English

A

aato gyararii *art gallery*
afutaasheebu rooshon *aftershave lotion*
ai *love*
ai suru *to love*
aishadoo *eye shadow*
aiteiru *open*
aka *red*
amai *sweet*
ao *blue*
arerugii *allergy*
asobu *play*
asupirin *aspirin*
atsui *hot*

B

bakkupakku *backpack*
basu *bus*
basuketto booru *basketball*
basutaoru *bath towel*
bataa *butter*
bejitarian *vegetarian*
biichi *beach*
biiru *beer*
bikini *bikini*
bikini-wakkusu *bikini wax*
bin *bottle*
bitaminzai *vitamin*
bochi *cemetery*
bokusaa-shootsu *boxers*

booi-furendo *boyfriend*
bookoo *attack*
booshi *cap*
burajaa *bra*
buriifu *briefs*
buta-niku *pork*
byoki *sick*
byuffe *buffet*

C

caado *card*
CD pureeyaa *CD player*
chairo *brown*
chichi *father*
chiimu *team*
chikai *near (nearby)*
chikatetsu *subway*
chiketto *ticket*
chikubi *nipple*
chizu *map*
chokoreeto *chocolate*
chooshoku *breakfast*
chuushoku *lunch*
cyuumon suru *to order*

D

daburu ruumu *double room*
dansu *to dance*
dansu-kurabu *dance club*
dejitaru kamera *digital camera*
denchi *battery*
denki *light*
densha *train*
denwa *phone*

denwa *phone*
denwa *telephone*
denwa suru *to phone*
denwa-bokkusu *phone booth*
deodoranto *deodorant*
depaato *department store*
doa *door*
doko *where*
dono *which*
donoyooni *how*
dorama *drama*
dorekurai *how long (time)*
doresu *dress*
doroboo *thief*
dozo *please*
DSL intaanetto akusesu
  DSL internet access

E

eakon *air conditioning*
ebi *shrimp*
ehagaki *postcard*
eiga *movie*
eiga-kan *theater*
eigo *English (language)*
eki *station*
enbun *sodium*

F

fandeeshon *foundation (make-up)*
feisharu *facial*
fittonesu-baiku *fitness bike*
fukikae *dubbed*
fuku *clothes*
fukumareru *included*

furaido-poteto *fries*
furaito *flight*
furii-maaketto *flea market*
furuutsu *fruit*
futsuka-yoi *hangover*

G

gaaru-furendo *girlfriend*
gaikoku *foreign*
gakusei *student*
gasorin *gas (gasoline)*
geeto *gate (at airport)*
gei *gay*
**genkin jidoo azukeire shiharaiki
  (ATM)** *cash machine (ATM)*
genkin ni kaeru
  to cash (a check)
geri *diarrhea*
gootoo *mugging*
gurasu *glass*
gureepu-furuutsu *grapefruit*
gyararii *gallery galerie*
gyuu-niku *beef*

H

haha *mother*
hai *yes*
hai-iro *gray*
hajimaru *to start*
haku *to barf*
hakubutsukan *museum*
hamigakiko *toothpaste*
hana *nose*
hanasu *to speak*
hankagai *downtown*

harau *to pay*
hataraku *to work*
henkin *refund*
heso *belly button*
heya *room*
hiitaa *heat (in building)*
hima *free (available)*
hitsuyoo ga aru *to need*
hiyake *sunburn*
hiyakedome *sun block*
hiyakerooshon *suntan lotion*
hoken *insurance*
hon *book*
hon-ya *bookstore*
hoomu *platform*
hoomupeeji *webpage page*
hooseki *jewelry*
hoteru *hotel*
hotto chokoreeto *hot chocolate*
hyoshiki *sign*

I

i *stomach*
i no fucho *upset stomach*
ichi *one*
ichi-jikan ni tsuki *per hour*
ichinichi *a day / one day*
ichi-nichi ni tsuki *per day*
ii *good*
iie *no*
ikura *how much*
ima *now*
intaanetto akusesu *internet access*

intaa'netto-kafe *internet café*
ippai *shot (of liquor)*
ippai ni suru *to fill*
irezumi *to tattoo*
Isha *doctor*
ishuukan ni tsuki *per week*
itamidome *painkiller*
itsu *when*
iyahoon *earphones*
iyana yatsu *scumbag*

J

jaketto *jacket*
jamu *jam*
jetto-sukii *jet ski*
jiinzu *jeans*
jikan *hour*
jikan *time*
jiko *accident*
jikokuhyo *schedule*
jimaku *subtitle*
jimusho *office*
jintonikku *gin and tonic*
jitensha *bicycle*
jogingu suru *to jog*
joohoo *information*
jyuusho *address*
jyuusu *juice*

K

kafe *café*
kafunsho *hay fever*
kagaku *science*
kagi *key*
kagi *lock*

kagi wo kakeru *to lock*

kajino *casino*

kaku *to write*

kakunin suru *to confirm*

kamera *camera*

kamera-ten *camera shop*

kamisori *razor*

kanjoo *check (in a restaurant)*

kanjoo-gaki *bill*

kankoo tsuaa *sightseeing tour*

kankooan'naijo *tourist information office*

kanshi-in *lifeguard*

kappu *cup*

karafu *carafe*

kariru *to rent*

karorii *calorie*

kasa *umbrella*

katamichi *one-way (ticket)*

kau *to buy*

kazoku *family*

keisatsu *police*

keisatsu *police station*

keishoku sutando *snack bar*

kenkooshokuhin-ten *health food store*

kensa *check*

keshoohin uriba *cosmetics department*

kiiro *yellow*

kin'en eria *non-smoking area*

kinenhi *memorial*

kin'enseki *smoking (section)*

kinko *safe*

kinkyuu *emergency*

kisu *kiss*

kisu suru *to kiss*

kitte *stamp (postage)*

koko *here*

kokusai gakusei shoo *International Student Card*

komedi *comedy*

kondishonaa *conditioner*

kondoomu *condom*

konpyuutaa *computer*

konsaato *concert*

kon'ya *tonight*

koocya *tea*

koohii *coffee*

kookan suru *to exchange*

kookuu-bin *airmail*

kookyo *palace*

koosha *kosher*

kooto *coat*

korekutokooru *collect call*

koresuterooru *cholesterol*

kowareru *to break*

kowareru *damaged*

kozutsumi *package*

kuchibeni *lipstick*

kuchibiru *lips*

kurejitto kaado *credit card*

kuro *black*

kuruma *car*

(naito) kurabu *(night) club*

kutsu *shoe*

kuukoo *airport*
kyoo *today*
kyoodai *brother*
kyookai *church*

M

machi *town*
machi no cyuushin *center of town*
machigai *mistake*
mado *window*
maguro *tuna*
maireeji *mileage*
makura *pillow*
manikyua *manicure*
matsu *to wait*
mayou *lost*
mayu *eyebrow*
mazui *disgusting (awful taste)*
me *eye*
meeru-adoresu *e-mail address*
memori-caado *memory card*
midori *green*
mineraru-wootaa *mineral water*
miru *to look (see)*
miru *watch*
miruku *milk*
mise *shop*
mise *store*
mitsuketa *found*
miyage *souvenir*
mizu *water*
moisuchaa *moisturizing*
moofu *blanket*

mootaa booto *motorboat*
mopetto *moped*
Motsu *to keep*
MP3 pureeyaa *MP3 player*
mu-guruten *gluten-free*
murasaki *purple*
mushi *bug*
mushi *insect*

N

nagai *long*
naito-kurabu *nightclub*
nama-biiru *draft (beer)*
nanji *what time*
napukin *napkin*
nashi de *without*
ni *two*
niwa *garden*
nodo *throat*
nodo no itami *sore throat*
nomimono *drink*
nomu *to drink*
norimono yoi *motion sickness*
nusumareru *stolen*
nuudisuto biichi *nude beach*
nyuujoo *entrance*

O

ofuro *bathroom*
ofuro *bath*
oishii *delicious*
okane *money*
okiniiri *favorite*
okureru *delay*
okureru *late*

ongaku *music*

oofuku *round-trip*

ookii *big*

ootomachikku *automatic*

orenji *orange*

oriru *to get off (a bus, train, etc.)*

otsuri *change*

oya *parent*

oyogu *to swim*

P

pan *bread*

pantsu *pants*

paudaa *powder*

pedikyua *pedicure*

pessarii *diaphragm*

pinku *pink*

piru *pill*

puroguramu *program*

puuru *swimming pool*

R

reeto *rate*

refurii *referee*

reipu *rape*

reji *cash register*

rekkaa sha *tow truck*

reshiito *receipt*

resutoran *restaurant*

rezu *lesbian*

ringo *apple*

rippugurosu *lip gloss*

rogu-on *to log on (computer)*

rooingu-mashiin *rowing machine*

rooraabureedo *to rollerblade*

roorupan *roll (bread)*

rosen *line*

ruumu saabisu *room service*

ryokoo *trip*

ryoogaejo *currency exchange office*

ryoojikan *consulate*

ryori suru *to cook*

S

saabisu *service*

saafin o suru *to surf*

saafuboodo *surfboard*

saba *mackerel*

saifu *wallet*

saigo *last*

saikuringu *cycling*

saisho *first*

saishoku shugisha *vegan*

sakaya *liquor store*

sakkaa *soccer*

sakkin kuriimu *antiseptic cream*

sangurasu *sunglasses*

sara *plate*

seeru-hin *on sale*

seeru-hin *sale*

seibishi *mechanic*

seikei-shujutsu *plastic surgery*

seiketsu *clean*

seiriyoo-napukin *sanitary napkin*

seki *cough*

seki *seat*

sekken *soap*

senpuuki *fan*

settoo *theft*

shanpuu *shampoo*

shashin *photo*

shatsu *shirt*

shawaa *shower*

shiai *(sports) game*

shiboo *fat*

shicyakushitsu *fitting room*

shimai *sister*

shimaru *to close*

shinbun-uriba *newsstand*

shingu *bedding*

shiro *castle*

shiro *white*

shitamachi *old town*

shiyakusho *town hall*

shohoo sen *prescription*

shokubutsuen *botanical garden*

shokuji *meal*

shooto-pantsu *shorts*

shoppingu sentaa *mall*

shoppingu-eria *shopping area*

shu *week*

shuppatsu suru *to leave*

shuuyaeigyou no yakkyoku *all-night pharmacy*

singuru ruumu *single room*

sokkusu *socks*

sokutatsu-bin *express mail*

soosu *sauce*

soto *outside*

subarashii *brilliant*

suicchi o ireru *to turn on (a machine)*

suiei-pantsu *swim trunks*

suijoo-sukii *waterski*

sukaato *skirt*

sukeetoboodo *to skateboard*

sukuryuu-doraibaa *screwdriver (alcoholic drink)*

superingu wo kaku *to spell*

supootsu-yoohin-ten *sports store*

susumeru *to recommend*

sutereo *stereo*

suupu *soup*

suutsukeesu *suitcase*

T

tabako *cigarette*

tabako o suu *to smoke*

tabemono *food*

taberu *to eat*

tadashii *right*

taito *tight*

taiyo *sun*

takai *expensive*

takushii *taxi*

tamago *egg*

tanpon *tampon*

taoru *towel*

T-baggu *thong*

tegami *letter*

tenisu *tennis*

terebi *television*

terefon-kaado *telephone card*

tisshu-peepaa *tissues*
todokede o suru *to report (to police)*
toire *restroom / toilet*
toiretto-peepaa *toilet paper*
tomeru *to stop*
tomodachi *friend*
tooi *far*
toonyoo byoo *diabetic*
tooroku *register*
toosuto *toast*
toraberaazu chekku *travelers checks*
torakku *truck*
toreddo-miru *treadmill*
tori-niku *chicken*
toru *to take (something)*
tou *tower*
toucyaku suru *to arrive*
t-shatsu *T-shirt*
tsuaa *tour*
tsugi *next*
tsukaisute kamera *disposable camera*
tsukareta *tired*
tsumetai *cold*
tsureteiku *to take (somewhere)*
tsuuka *currency*

U

unchin *fare*
uriba *department (in store)*
utsukushii *beautiful*

V

vareebooru *volleyball*

W

wain *wine*
wain *wine*
wakarimasu *to understand*
waribiki *discount*
warui *bad*

Y

yakkyoku *pharmacy*
yakusu *to translate*
yoru *night*
yoyaku *reservation*
yoyaku o toru *to reserve*
yukkuri *slowly*
yuubin-kyoku *post office*
yuubin-ryookin *postage*
yuugata *evening*
yuushoku *dinner*

Z

zei *duty (tax)*
zei *tax*
zensai *appetizer*

DICTIONARY
English > Japanese

A

accident *jiko*
address *jyuusho*
aftershave lotion *afutaasheebu rooshon*
air conditioning *eakon*
airmail *kookuu-bin*
airport *kuukoo*
allergy *arerugii*
all-night pharmacy *shuuyaeigyou no yakkyoku*
antiseptic cream *sakkin kuriimu*
appetizer *zensai*
apple *ringo*
to arrive *toucyaku suru*
art gallery *aato gyararii*
aspirin *asupirin*
ATM (cash machine) *genkin jidoo azukeire shiharaiki*
attack *bookoo*
automatic *ootomachikku*

B

backpack *bakkupakku*
bad *warui*
to barf *haku*
basketball *basuketto booru*
bath *ofuro*
bath towel *basutaoru*
bathroom *ofuro*

battery *denchi*
beach *biichi*
beautiful *utsukushii*
bedding *shingu*
beef *gyuu-niku*
beer *biiru*
belly button *heso*
bicycle *jitensha*
big *ookii*
bikini *bikini*
bikini wax *bikini-wakkusu*
bill *kanjoo-gaki*
black *kuro*
blanket *moofu*
blue *ao*
book *hon*
bookstore *hon-ya*
botanical garden *shokubutsuen*
bottle *bin*
boxers *bokusaa-shootsu*
boyfriend *booi-furendo*
bra *burajaa*
bread *pan*
to break *kowareru*
breakfast *chooshoku*
briefs *buriifu*
brilliant *subarashii*
brother *kyoodai*
brown *chairo*
buffet *byuffe*
bug *mushi*
bus *basu*
butter *bataa*
to buy *kau*

C

café *kafe*
calorie *karorii*
camera *kamera*
camera shop *kamera-ten*
cap *booshi*
car *kuruma*
carafe *karafu*
card *caado*
to cash (a check) *genkin ni kaeru*
cash machine (ATM) *genkin jidoo azukeire shiharaiki (ATM)*
cash register *reji*
casino *kajino*
castle *shiro*
CD player *CD pureeyaa*
cemetery *bochi*
center of town *machi no cyuushin*
change *otsuri*
check *kensa*
check (in a restaurant) *kanjoo*
chicken *tori-niku*
chocolate *chokoreeto*
cholesterol *koresuterooru*
church *kyookai*
cigarette *tabako*
clean *seiketsu*
to close *shimaru*
clothes *fuku*
(night) club *(naito) kurabu*
coat *kooto*
coffee *koohii*
cold *tsumetai*
collect call *korekutokooru*

comedy *komedi*
computer *konpyuutaa*
concert *konsaato*
conditioner *kondishonaa*
condom *kondoomu*
to confirm *kakunin suru*
consulate *ryoojikan*
to cook *ryori suru*
cosmetics department *keshoohin uriba*
cough *seki*
credit card *kurejitto kaado*
cup *kappu*
currency *tsuuka*
currency exchange office *ryoogaejo*
cycling *saikuringu*

D

damaged *kowareru*
dance club *dansu-kurabu*
to dance *dansu*
day *hi / nichi*
delay *okureru*
delicious *oishii*
deodorant *deodoranto*
department (in store) *uriba*
department store *depaato*
diabetic *toonyoo byoo*
diaphragm *pessarii*
diarrhea *geri*
digital camera *dejitaru kamera*
dinner *yuushoku*
discount *waribiki*

disgusting (awful taste) *mazui*

disposable camera *tsukaisute kamera*

doctor *Isha*

door *doa*

double room *daburu ruumu*

downtown *hankagai*

draft (beer) *nama-biiru*

drama *dorama*

dress *doresu*

drink *nomimono*

to drink *nomu*

DSL internet access *DSL intaanetto akusesu*

dubbed *fukikae*

duty (tax) *zei*

E

earphones *iyahoon*

to eat *taberu*

egg *tamago*

e-mail address *meeru-adoresu*

emergency *kinkyuu*

English (language) *eigo*

entrance *nyuujoo*

evening *yuugata*

to exchange *kookan suru*

expensive *takai*

express mail *sokutatsu-bin*

eye *me*

eye shadow *aishadoo*

eyebrow *mayu*

F

facial *feisharu*

family *kazoku*

fan *senpuuki*

far *tooi*

fare *unchin*

fat *shiboo*

father *chichi*

favorite *okiniiri*

to fill *ippai ni suru*

first *saisho*

fitness bike *fittonesu-baiku*

fitting room *shicyakushitsu*

flea market *furii-maaketto*

flight *furaito*

food *tabemono*

foreign *gaikoku*

found *mitsuketa*

foundation (make-up) *fandeeshon*

free (available) *hima*

friend *tomodachi*

fries *furaido-poteto*

fruit *furuutsu*

G

gallery galerie *gyararii*

(sports) game *shiai*

garden *niwa*

gas (gasoline) *gasorin*

gate (at airport) *geeto*

gay *gei*

to get off (a bus, train, etc.) *oriru*

gin and tonic *jintonikku*
girlfriend *gaaru-furendo*
glass *gurasu*
gluten-free *mu-guruten*
good *ii*
grapefruit *gureepu-furuutsu*
gray *hai-iro*
green *midori*

H

hangover *futsuka-yoi*
hay fever *kafunsho*
health food store *kenkooshokuhin-ten*
heat (in building) *hiitaa*
here *koko*
hot *atsui*
hot chocolate *hotto chokoreeto*
hotel *hoteru*
hour *jikan*
how *donoyooni*
how long (time) *dorekurai*
how much *ikura*

I

included *fukumareru*
information *joohoo*
insect *mushi*
insurance *hoken*
International Student Card *kokusai gakusei shoo*
internet access *intaanetto akusesu*
internet café *intaa'netto-kafe*

J

jacket *jaketto*
jam *jamu*
jeans *jiinzu*
jet ski *jetto-sukii*
jewelry *hooseki*
to jog *jogingu suru*
juice *jyuusu*

K

to keep *motsu*
key *kagi*
kiss *kisu*
to kiss *kisu suru*
kosher *koosha*

L

last *saigo*
late *okureru*
to leave *shuppatsu suru*
lesbian *rezu*
letter *tegami*
lifeguard *kanshi-in*
light *denki*
line *rosen*
lip gloss *rippugurosu*
lips *kuchibiru*
lipstick *kuchibeni*
liquor store *sakaya*
lock *kagi*
to lock *kagi wo kakeru*
to log on (computer) *rogu-on*
long *nagai*
to look (see) *miru*

lost *mayou*
love *ai*
to love *ai suru*
lunch *chuushoku*

M

mackerel *saba*
mall *shoppingu sentaa*
manicure *manikyua*
map *chizu*
meal *shokuji*
mechanic *seibishi*
memorial *kinenhi*
memory card *memori-caado*
mileage *maireeji*
milk *miruku*
mineral water *mineraru-wootaa*
mistake *machigai*
moisturizing *moisuchaa*
money *okane*
moped *mopetto*
mother *haha*
motion sickness *norimono yoi*
motorboat *mootaa booto*
movie *eiga*
MP3 player *MP3 pureeyaa*
mugging *gootoo*
museum *hakubutsukan*
music *ongaku*

N

napkin *napukin*
near (nearby) *chikai*
to need *hitsuyoo ga aru*

newsstand *shinbun-uriba*
next *tsugi*
night *yoru*
nightclub *naito-kurabu*
nipple *chikubi*
no *iie*
non-smoking area *kin'en eria*
nose *hana*
now *ima*
nude beach *nuudisuto biichi*

O

office *jimusho*
old town *shitamachi*
on sale *seeru-hin*
one *ichi*
one-way (ticket) *katamichi*
open *aiteiru*
orange *orenji*
to order *cyuumon suru*
outside *soto*

P

package *kozutsumi*
painkiller *itamidome*
palace *kookyo*
pants *pantsu*
parent *oya*
to pay *harau*
pedicure *pedikyua*
per day *ichi-nichi ni tsuki*
per hour *ichi-jikan ni tsuki*
per week *ishuukan ni tsuki*
pharmacy *yakkyoku*

phone *denwa*
to phone *denwa suru*
phone booth *denwa-bokkusu*
photo *shashin*
pill *piru*
pillow *makura*
pink *pinku*
plastic surgery *seikei-shujutsu*
plate *sara*
platform *hoomu*
play *asobu*
please *dozo*
police *keisatsu*
police station *keisatsu*
pork *buta-niku*
post office *yuubin-kyoku*
postage *yuubin-ryookin*
postcard *ehagaki*
powder *paudaa*
prescription *shohoo sen*
program *puroguramu*
purple *murasaki*

R

rape *reipu*
rate *reeto*
razor *kamisori*
receipt *reshiito*
to recommend *susumeru*
red *aka*
referee *refurii*
refund *henkin*
register *tooroku*

to rent *kariru*
to report (to police) *todokede o suru*
reservation *yoyaku*
to reserve *yoyaku o toru*
restaurant *resutoran*
restroom *toire*
right *tadashii*
to rollerblade *rooraabureedo*
roll (bread) *roorupan*
room *heya*
room service *ruumu saabisu*
round-trip *oofuku*
rowing machine *rooingu-mashiin*

S

safe *kinko*
sale *seeru-hin*
sanitary napkin *seiriyoo-napukin*
sauce *soosu*
schedule *jikokuhyo*
science *kagaku*
screwdriver (alcoholic drink) *sukuryuu-doraibaa*
scumbag *iyana yatsu*
seat *seki*
service *saabisu*
shampoo *shanpuu*
shirt *shatsu*
shoe *kutsu*
shop *mise*
shopping area *shoppingu-eria*
shorts *shooto-pantsu*

shot (of liquor) *ippai*

shower *shawaa*

shrimp *ebi*

sick *byoki*

sightseeing tour *kankoo tsuaa*

sign *hyoshiki*

single room *singuru ruumu*

sister *shimai*

skirt *sukaato*

slowly *yukkuri*

to smoke *tabako o suu*

smoking (section) *kin'enseki*

snack bar *keishoku sutando*

soap *sekken*

soccer *sakkaa*

socks *sokkusu*

sodium *enbun*

sore throat *nodo no itami*

soup *suupu*

souvenir *miyage*

to speak *hanasu*

to spell *superingu wo kaku*

sports store *supootsu-yoohin-ten*

stamp (postage) *kitte*

to start *hajimaru*

station *eki*

stereo *sutereo*

stolen *nusumareru*

stomach *i*

to stop *tomeru*

store *mise*

student *gakusei*

subtitle *jimaku*

subway *chikatetsu*

suitcase *suutsukeesu*

sun *taiyo*

sun block *hiyakedome*

sunburn *hiyake*

sunglasses *sangurasu*

suntan lotion *hiyakerooshon*

to surf *saafin o suru*

surfboard *saafuboodo*

sweet *amai*

to swim *oyogu*

swim trunks *suiei-pantsu*

swimming pool *puuru*

T

to take (something) *toru*

to take (somewhere) *tsureteiku*

tampon *tanpon*

to tattoo *irezumi*

tax *zei*

taxi *takushii*

tea *koocya*

team *chiimu*

telephone *denwa*

telephone card *terefon-kaado*

television *terebi*

tennis *tenisu*

theater *eiga-kan*

theft *settoo*

thief *doroboo*

thong *T-baggu*

throat *nodo*

ticket *chiketto*

133

tight *taito*	**U**
time *jikan*	**umbrella** *kasa*
tired *tsukareta*	**to understand** *wakarimasu*
tissues *tisshu-peepaa*	**upset stomach** *i no fucho*
toast *toosuto*	**V**
today *kyoo*	
toilet *toire*	**vegan** *saishoku shugisha*
toilet paper *toiretto-peepaa*	**vegetarian** *bejitarian*
tonight *kon'ya*	**vitamin** *bitaminzai*
toothpaste *hamigakiko*	**volleyball** *vareebooru*
tour *tsuaa*	**W**
tourist information office *kankooan'naijo*	**to wait** *matsu*
tow truck *rekkaa sha*	**wallet** *saifu*
towel *taoru*	**war memorial** *(sensoo) kinenhi*
tower *tou*	**watch** *miru*
town *machi*	**water** *mizu*
town hall *shiyakusho*	**waterski** *suijoo-sukii*
train *densha*	**webpage page** *hoomupeeji*
to translate *yakusu*	**week** *shu*
travelers checks *toraberaazu chekku*	**what time** *nanji*
treadmill *toreddo-miru*	**when** *itsu*
trip *ryokoo*	**where** *doko*
truck *torakku*	**which** *dono*
T-shirt *t-shatsu*	**white** *shiro*
tuna *maguro*	**window** *mado*
to turn on (a machine) *suicchi o ireru*	**wine** *wain*
two *ni*	**wine** *wain*
	without *nashi de*
	to work *hataraku*
	to write *kaku*

Y

yellow *kiiro*
yes *hai*